The British TV Field Guide

from

IHeartBritishTV.com

Written By:

Stefanie Hutson
David Ford
Charles Hutson

Published by IHeartBritishTV.com
Sacramento, California

ISBN: 978-0-578-21370-5

Printed in the United States of America

For Jo & Judy, two of our favorite British TV fans

AND

To British TV fans everywhere, for being such a delightful group of people

TABLE OF CONTENTS

INTRODUCTION

Welcome! First off, I want to say thank you for purchasing this book. In doing so, you're supporting a small business and enabling us to spend more time creating content and resources for British TV fans. We appreciate you!

The guide before you is designed to act as a companion for your British TV viewing. We wanted to create something that would help people discover new shows while also tracking shows and seasons watched.

There have been so many times we've started watching something only to realize (often with great disappointment) we've seen it before. With roughly 1700 shows and places to check off seasons as you finish them, this should help that problem.

For all it's benefits, though, the British TV Field Guide is not an encyclopedia. There will certainly be shows or specials we missed, especially when it comes to older or rarer titles.

Many were omitted intentionally because they're not available even on DVD, or they were deleted from the archives, or they never made it past the pilot stage. We also excluded game shows, talk shows, one-off specials, and most children's programming (with some exceptions for outstanding young adult series).

If we've missed something you feel should be included, or if you find mistakes, please feel free to email them to stefanie@iheartbritishtv.com or david@iheartbritishtv.com.

Thank you, and happy watching!

The IHeartBritishTV.com Team

THE GUIDE TO THE GUIDE

While most of this guide should be pretty self-explanatory, we wanted to clear up a few things that might be confusing.

TITLES

When titles started with "A" or "The", we alphabetized them with the leading word. You'll find The Night Manager under the "T" section, not N.

Also, keep in mind that many shows have multiple titles. For example, the show known as "C.B. Strike" in the US is simply "Strike" in the UK. We've tried to opt for the name we hear used more frequently.

DATES

Dates for recent shows can be a bit tricky. Where possible, we listed the last air year and only included a closing year where there's word of cancellation or a lack of news about new seasons after 2-3+ years. Still, some shows are brought back from the dead, and others can be cancelled unexpectedly.

SEASONS & SPECIALS

You may notice some shows are listed with extra seasons. Those are cases where a season has been ordered but not yet released.

If you see a show with an "M", that means it was a miniseries. But remember - some shows are created as a miniseries until they become wildly successful and the creator is asked to continue the story.

CATEGORIES

While we did our best to categorize shows, some have strong crossover between multiple categories (particularly drama/comedy and drama/mystery). If you don't see something in the section you think is most appropriate, try the next most likely.

15 Storeys High - 2002 to 2004 - Two flatmates live in a fifteenth floor flat. Errol is simple and likeable, while Vince is nasty and grouchy. 1___ 2___

2point4 Children - 1991 to 1999 - An average family with two children has more than their share of bad luck. 1___ 2___ 3___ 4___ 5___ 6___ 7___ 8___ | Christmas Specials: 92___ 93___ 94___ 95___ 96___

A Bear's Tail - 2005 - A talking bear lives with an eccentric sitcom family. 1___

A Bit of a Do - 1989 - This sitcom follows the lives of the working class Simcocks and the middle class Rodenhursts at various social functions. 1___ 2___

A Class by Himself - 1971 to 1972 - An eccentric nobleman in Somerset falls on hard times. 1___

A Fine Romance - 1981 to 1984 - Dame Judi Dench and her late husband star in this sitcom about two socially awkward adults who fall in love. 1___ 2___ 3___ 4___

A Gentleman's Club - 1988 - It's chaos when a woman is hired on as secretary in a male-dominated institution. 1___

A Gert Lush Christmas - 2015 - This one-off Christmas TV movie about an eccentric family Christmas in Bristol could come back as a series, should the actors find the time. M___

A Kind of Living - 1988 to 1990 - Richard Griffiths stars as a man with a new job, a new baby, and a mind that's somewhere else. 1___ 2___ 3___

A Many Splintered Thing - 2000 - Alan Davies stars as a wannabe composer who writes radio jingles. After an unhappy binge, he embarks on an affair. 1___

A Perfect State - 1997 - A small coastal town in England realizes it was never officially annexed into the United Kingdom and declares itself an independent state. 1___

A Prince Among Men - 1997 to 1998 - An aggravating man struggles with too much talent and not enough humility. 1___ 2___

A Sharp Intake of Breath - 1977 to 1981 - Easygoing Peter deals with life's frustrations in his own careless and whimsical way. 1___ 2___ 3___ 4___

A Small Problem - 1987 - In an alternate Britain, people less than 5 feet tall are banished to a ghetto. 1___

A Very Peculiar Practice - 1986 to 1988 - A young doctor treats a wide variety of patients at a university health center. 1___ 2___ | Spinoff Movie: A Very Polish Practice ___

About Face - 1989 to 1991 - Actress

Maureen Lipman plays different roles in unconnected episodes with different special guests. 1__ 2__

Absolute Power - 2003 to 2005 - Prentiss McCabe works for a PR firm that will do whatever it takes to promote their clients. 1__ 2__

Absolutely Fabulous - 2001 to 2012 - Two wild middle-aged women do everything but act their age. 1__ 2__ 3__ 4__ 5__ | Specials: The Last Shout 1__ 2__ Gay__ Christmas Special 2004__ 20th Anniversary Specials 1__ 2__ 3__ Comic Relief 2005__ Sport Relief 2012__ Absolutely Fabulous: The Movie__

According to Bex - 2005 - Bex Atwell is a young woman with everything she wants just a little out of her grasp. 1__

Action Team - 2018 to present - This spoof comedy follows the activities of a special branch of MI6. 1__

Adam's Family Tree - 1997 to 1999 - In this children's comedy, Adam is able to summon help from his ancestors whenever he needs it. 1__ 2__ 3__

Adrian Mole: The Cappuccino Years - 2001 - Stephen Mangan (*Dirk Gently*) and Alison Steadman (*Gavin & Stacey*) star in this adaptation of Sue Townsend's book in which Adrian Mole struggles with adult life. 1__

Affairs of the Heart - 1983 to 1985 - After surviving a heart attack, a man stops living. 1__

After Henry - 1988 to 1992 - Sarah shares a house with her mother and daughter. After her husband dies, they have to find a way to get along. 1__ 2__ 3__ 4__

After Hours - 2015 - After heartbreak and watching his friends go on to uni, a young man takes solace in an internet radio station. 1__

After You've Gone - 2007 to 2008 - After his wife decides to leave him and move to Africa, Jimmy has to find a way to manage his kids and his mother-in-law. 1__ 2__ 3__

Agony - 1979 to 1981 - Jane has a call-in radio show to help solve people's troubles, but she's not much good with her own. 1__ 2__ 3__

Agony Again - 1995 - This follow-up to *Agony* shows Jane Lucas once again struggling with her own problems while she focuses on everyone else's. 1__

Ain't Misbehavin' - 1997 - Two bandsmen enjoy themselves in wartime London. 1__

Ain't Misbehavin' - 1994 to 1995 - When Sonia tells Clive their spouses are having an affair, it sets into motion a wild chain of events. 1__ 2__

AJ Wentworth BA - 1982 - In 1940s England, a maths teacher deals with school issues. 1__

Alas Smith & Jones - 1984 to 1988 - Smith and Jones do short sketches about modern life, many of which are in poor taste. 1__ 2__ 3__ 4__ | Christmas Specials: 1987__ 1988__

Alcock & Gander - 1972 - After her

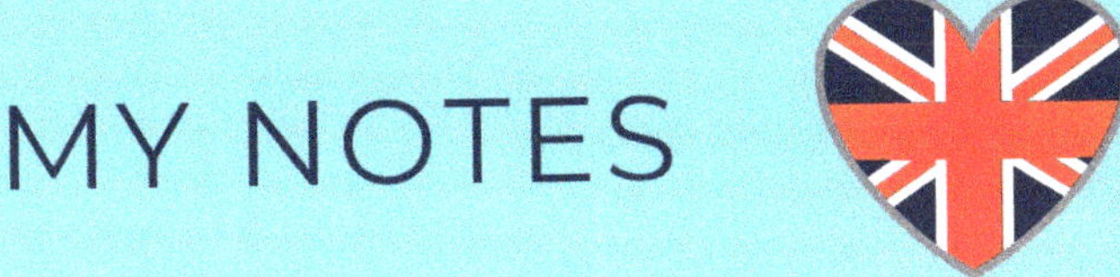
MY NOTES

husband's death, Marigold Alcock inherits his businesses. 1__

Alfresco - 1983 to 1984 - This early-80s variety show is packed with now-famous actors like Emma Thompson, Robbie Coltrane, Hugh Laurie, and Stephen Fry. 1__ 2__

All About Me - 2002 to 2004 - This sitcom features a multicultural blended family living in Birmingham with a special needs child. 1__ 2__ 3__

All Along the Watchtower - 1999 - Two men watch over a Cold War radar station, but the Cold War is over. 1__

All at Number 20 - 1986 to 1987 - When a woman's husband dies without life insurance, she takes on lodgers to help keep their home. 1__ 2__

All Gas & Gaiters - 1966 to 1971 - A hapless curate is the butt of clerical humour. 1__ 2__ 3__ 4__ 5__ | Christmas Night with the Stars Special__

All in Good Faith - 1985 to 1988 - Middle-aged Reverend Philip Lambe decides to relocate from rural Oxfordshire to an urban Midlands parish, inheriting a whole new set of issues. 1__ 2__ 3__

All Night Long - 1994 - Bill Chivers learns to bake in prison and hopes to go straight. 1__ | 1988 Special__

All Quiet on the Preston Front - 1994 to 1997 - This Lancashire-based comedy features the misadventures of a group of friends in a local unit of the Territorial Army. 1__ 2__ 3__

Allo 'Allo - 1982 to 1992 - This classic British comedy is set in a French café during WWII. 1__ 2__ 3__ 4__ 5__ 6__ 7__ 8__ 9__ | The Best of 'Allo 'Allo__ The Return of 'Allo 'Allo__

Ambassadors - 2013 - Mitchell and Webb star in this miniseries about a British ambassador to a fictional Asian country. M__

An Actor's Life for Me - 1991 - An eternally optimistic actor always seems to think his big break is around the corner. 1__

An Idiot Abroad - 2010 to 2012 - Two friends send Karl, a man who's never travelled outside of England, to unfamiliar cultures to see what happens. 1__ 2__ 3__

And Mother Makes Five... - 1974 to 1976 - This spinoff is essentially a continuation of the popular 70s sitcom And Mother Makes Three... 1__ 2__ 3__ 4__

And Mother Makes Three... - 1971 to 1973 - A newly widowed mother does her best to raise her children and hold down a job with the local veterinarian.1__ 2__ 3__ 4__ | 1971 Special__

Andy Capp - 1988 - Andy drinks, follows the horses, and lets his wife be the breadwinner. 1__

Angelo's - 2007 to 2007 - Miranda Hart appears in this quirky comedy about a greasy spoon in London. 1__

Are You Being Served? - 1972 to 1985 - At the Grace Brothers Department Store, fine fashions are served with a healthy side of mischief. 1__ 2__ 3__ 4__ 5__ 6__ 7__

8___ 9___ 10___ | Christmas Specials: 1975___ 1976___ 1978___ 1979___ 1981___ | 2016 Reboot Special___

Are You Being Served? Again! - 1992 to 1993 - When the Grace Brothers store is closed, the staff takes over managing a manor house in the countryside. 1___ 2___

As Time Goes By - 1992 to 2005 - Separated by war, lovers Lionel and Jean are reunited by chance many years later. 1___ 2___ 3___ 4___ 5___ 6___ 7___ 8___ 9___ 10___ | 2002 Compilation Special___ | 2005 Reunion Specials: 1___ 2___

Asylum - 2015 - Two men are trapped together in a London embassy in order to avoid extradition. M___

Atletico Partick - 1995 to 1996 - When Karen's husband Jack is more interested in football than her, she finds solace with Ally, a man more interested in sex than football. 1___

Auf Wiedersehen, Pet - 1983 to 2004 - This series looks at the lives of British workers thrown together in Germany. 1___ 2___ 3___ 4___ 5___ | Comic Relief Sketch___ | Au Revoir: 1___ 2___

Back - 2017 to present - After the death of their father, two estranged foster sons try to run the family business. 1___ 2___

Bad Education - 2012 to 2014 - In this school-based sitcom, the teacher is more of a kid than the students. 1___ 2___ 3___ | Movie___

Bad Move - 2017 to present - After a few too many episodes of Escape to the Country, Steve & Nicky decide to relocate from Leeds to the countryside...and quickly regret it. 1___

Baddiel's Syndrome - 2001 - An architect who suspects he might be Jewish seeks therapy. 1___

Badults - 2013 to 2014 - This sitcom is all about the crazy lives of three young male flatmates. 1___ 2___

Barbara - 1995 to 2003 - A no-nonsense housewife makes her family fearful of getting on her bad side. 1___ 2___ 3___

Beast - 2000 to 2001 - Alexander Armstrong stars as Nick, a country vet who doesn't particularly like animals (but who does love their attractive female caretakers). 1___ 2___

Bedtime - 2001 to 2003 - This comedy-drama revolves around the bedtime conversations of different couples. 1___ 2___ 3___

Being Eileen - 2011 to 2013 - Originally created as a Christmas special about a family traveling to Lapland during the holidays, this comedy drama later got a full season to continue the family's story. 1___

Believe Nothing - 2002 - When the cleverest man in Britain gets bored, he joins a shadowy organization that controls everything in the world. 1___

Benidorm - 2007 to 2018 - A parade of guests try to get their money's worth at a resort in Benidorm. 1___ 2___ 3___ 4___ 5___ 6___ 7___ 8___ 9___ 10___

Benny Hill Show - 1969 to 1989 - Benny

Hill plays different characters in occasionally smutty sketches 1__ 2__ 3__ 4__ 5__ 6__ 7__ 8__ 9__ 10__11__ 12__ 13__ 14__ 15__ 16__ 17__ 18__ 19__

Big Bad World - 2013 - Newly-graduated Ben is ready to take on the world, but it's not working out like he planned. 1__

Big School - 2013 to 2014 - A new French teacher arrives at Greybridge School and gives the long-time Deputy Head of Science second thoughts about resigning. 1__ 2__

Billy Liar - 1973 to 1974 - In this whimsical comedy, a young man works in a funeral parlour and spends far too much time daydreaming. 1__ 2__

Birds of a Feather - 1989 to 2018 - When their husbands are arrested for armed robbery, two women must figure out how to take care of themselves. 1__ 2__ 3__ 4__ 5__ 6__ 7__ 8__ 9__ 10__11__12__13__ | Christmas Specials: 1989__ 1990__ 1991__ 1992__ 1993__ 1994__ 1997__ 1998__ 2014__ 2016__ 2017__ | 1996 Flashback Special__

Blackadder - 1982 to 1987 - Prince Edmund the Black Adder spends his time thinking up ways to get the crown. 1__ 2__ 3__ 4__ | Specials: The Cavalier Years__ Blackadder's Christmas Carol__ Blackadder: Back and Forth__

Black Books - 2000 to 2004 - Bernard Black is not very good with the customers at his book store. 1__ 2__ 3__

Blandings - 2013 to 2014 - A nobleman struggles to keep his stately home and strange family in line so he can spend more time with his beloved pig. 1__ 2__

Bless Me Father - 1978 to 1981 - A veteran Irish Catholic priest tries to break in his young curate in post-war Britain with the help of some quirky characters and Catholic parish life crises. 1__ 2__ 3__

Bless This House - 1971 to 1976 - A traveling salesman and his wife love their teenagers, but they're hopelessly out of touch. 1__ 2__ 3__ 4__ 5__ 6__ | Movie__

Bliss - 2018 - Stephen Mangan plays a man living an exhausting double life. 1__

Bloomers - 1979 - A struggling young actor takes a job in a florist shop. 1__

Blue Heaven - 1992 to 1994 - Frank dreams that his singing team, Blue Heaven, can make it big in spite of his crazy home life. 1__

Bluestone 42 - 2013 to 2015 - This sitcom features stories about a bomb squad disposal unit in Afghanistan. 1__ 2__ 3__ | 2013 Christmas Special__

Bob Martin - 2000 to 2001 - About a daytime game show host, his troubles and his willingness to do whatever to get where he wants to be. 1__ 2__

Bob Servant - 2013 - When a highly unqualified and self-absorbed man wins a local political election, the area doesn't know what hit it. 1__

Bonjour la Classe - 1993 - A new French teacher arrives at a prestigious school to find himself disillusioned with the priorities of everyone there. 1___

Bonkers - 2007 - A fortysomething teacher's world is turned upside down when she finds out her long-time husband has been cheating on her. 1___

Boomers - 2014 to 2016 - Retired friends make comedy of learning to deal with retirement. 1✓ 2✓ | 2015 Christmas Special___?

Borderline - 2016 to 2017 - At a fictitious airport, an inept team of border patrol agents keeps England safe. 1___ 2___

Born and Bred - 2002 to 2005 - Chris Chibnall wrote this Lancashire-based comedy-drama about a man and his son running a small cottage hospital. 1___ 2___ 3___ 4___ | 2003 Christmas Special___

Bounty Hunters - 2017 to 2018 - Jack Whitehall and Rosie Perez star in this action comedy about a bookish Brit and a tough American Latina who enter into a partnership of sorts. 1___ 2___

Bowler - 1973 - Scheming Stanley Bowler lives with his controlling mother, drives a 'Mercaidis' and mispronounces words in this funny sitcom. 1___

Boy Meets Girl - 2015 to 2016 - Boy Meets Girl takes a look at love across "the transgender age gap". 1___ 2___

Brassic - 2019 to present - Brassic is another word for broke, and this series features a group of young working class friends living and struggling in Lancashire. 1___

Bread - 1986 to 1991 - The Boswell family lives very well on government handouts and cash jobs, but none of them are happy. 1___ 2___ 3___ 4___ 5___ 6___ 7___ | Christmas Specials: 1988___ 1989___ 1990___

Brotherly Love - 1999 - This sitcom is a bit like a Scottish version of Last of the Summer Wine. 1___

Brush Strokes - 1986 to 1991 - House painter Jacko has the greatest appreciation for all kinds of women. Will one of them turn out to be the right one for him? 1___ 2___ 3___ 4___ 5___

Bucket - 2017 to present - When free-spirited Mim tells her daughter she's dying, they go on a road trip together. 1___

Budgie - 1971 to 1972 - Optimistic 'Budgie' Bird is a failure at every con and moneymaking scheme he tries, and nobody can manage to set him straight. 1___ 2___

Bull - 2015 - Two woefully underqualified siblings try to run an antique shop together. 1___

Burnistoun - 2009 to 2012 - This Scottish sketch comedy is set in a fictional town near Glasgow. 1___ 2___ 3___

Butterflies - 1978 to 1983 - Housewife Ria's husband seems to pay more attention to his butterfly collection than her. 1___ 2___ 3___ 4___ | 1979 Christmas Special___ 1982 Christmas Sketch___ Children in Need Special___

Camping - 2016 - A simple birthday camping trip among friends turns tense. 1___

Campus - 2009 to 2011 - Cuts are coming, and the faculty at a fictitious British college scramble to save their positions. 1___

Carrie & Barry - 2004 to 2005 - This sitcom features stories about a London cabbie, his wife, and his partner who half owns the cab. 1___ 2___

Carters Get Rich - 2017 to present - An 11-year-old creates an app and sells it for 10 million pounds, changing his family's life forever. 1___

Cast Offs - 2009 - This mockumentary follows 6 disabled people sent to live on an island for a reality show. 1___

Catastrophe - 2015 to present - While in London on a business trip, Irish Sharon and American Rob have a fling with lasting consequences. 1___ 2___ 3___ 4___

Chalk - 1997 - This early work by Steven Moffat focuses on the chaotic environs of Galfast High. 1___ 2___

Chance in a Million - 1984 to 1986 - Tom Chance is forever caught in the middle of inconvenient coincidences. 1___ 2___ 3___

Chewin' the Fat - 1999 to 2005 - This Scottish sketch comedy is mostly set in Glasgow. 1___ 2___ 3___ 4___

Chewing Gum - 2015 to 2017 - This London-based sitcom features a religious 24-year-old shopgirl who wants to learn more about sex. 1___ 2___

Chickens - 2011 to 2013 - This period comedy is about 3 men who didn't go off to WWI and became outcasts in their village. 1___

Citizen Smith - 1977 to 1980 - An unemployed dreamer in London attempts to be like his idol, Che Guevara. 1___ 2___ 3___ 4___

City Lights - 1986 to 1991 - A Glasgow bank teller with dreams of writing finds himself constantly held back by the people in his life. 1___ 2___ 3___ 4___ 5___ 6___

City Lights - 2007 to 2008 - Robson Green and Mark Benton are best friends with an intense rivalry. 1___ | 2008 Christmas Special___

Clarence - 1988 - Clarence is a short-sighted delivery driver who spends most of his time bumping into things. 1___

Class Act - 1994 to 1995 - When a snobby rich woman's husband disappears with all her money, she has to learn how to take care of herself. 1___ 2___

Clone - 2008 - Dr. Victor attempts to create a clone that could replace humans in the

> Simon Callow, who starred alongside Brenda Blethyn in *Chance in a Million*, once said he believed his character's unusual speech patterns were inspired by Mr. Jingle in *The Pickwick Papers*.

army, but the results fall short of his expectations. 1___

Close to Home - 1989 to 1990 - A divorced North London veterinarian attempts to make a normal life for himself and his two teenagers, but it's often complicated by his ex. 1___ 2___

Colin's Sandwich - 1988 to 1990 - Colin is a complaint taker for British Railways, but he really wants to be a writer. 1___ 2___

Come Fly with Me - 2010 to 2011 - The cast of Little Britain parodies life in a British airport. 1___

Coming of Age - 2007 to 2011 - Five sixth form students come of age in Abingdon, Oxfordshire. 1___ 2___ 3___ | 2009 Comic Relief Spccial___

Count Arthur Strong - 2013 to 2017 - A delusional former actor tries to put together his life story with the help of a partner's son. 1___ 2___ 3___

Coupling - 2000 to 2004 - Six best friends deal with friendship, relationships and sex, sex, sex. 1___ 2___ 3___ 4___

Cowboys - 1980 to 1981 - Three shoddy builders put things together in a way that makes them last just long enough for them to get paid. 1___ 2___ 3___

Cradle to Grave - 2015 - Danny Baker and his friends grow up in 1970s South London. 1___

Crashing - 2016 - Six twenty and thirtysomething friends live in temporary spaces in abandoned buildings as an alternative to expensive London rental prices. 1___

Crazyhead - 2016 - 20-somethings work on becoming adults while also battling demons (real ones, not "personal demons") in this comedy. 1___

Cribbins - 1969 to 1970 - Bernard Cribbins stars in this classic sketch comedy. 1___ 2___

Crims - 2015 - Young Luke drives a getaway car for his friend and gets two years in the Young Offender Institution. 1___

Cuckoo - 2012 to 2018 - When a British woman brings an American hippie back home as her husband, they aren't terribly well-received by her proper British family. 1___ 2___ 3___ 4___

Cunk on Britain - 2018 to present - Reporter Philomena Cunk asks the big questions about politics, history, art, and society. 1___

Curry & Chips - 1969 - This controversial comedy features a darkened Spike Milligan playing an Asian immigrant, and was removed from television after just six episodes. 1___

Dad's Army - 1968 to 1977 - This classic British comedy focuses on Home Guard volunteers preparing for German invasion during WWII. 1___ 2___ 3___ 4___ 5___ 6___ 7___ 8___ 9___ | Christmas Specials: 1971___ 1975___ | October 1976 Special___ | Christmas Night with the Stars Sketches: 1968___ 1969___ 1970___ 1972___ | 1971 Movie___ 2016 Movie___

Damned - 2016 to present - Alan Davies

(*Jonathan Creek*) stars in this series about workers in a social services department. 1___ 2___

Dead Boss - 2012 - Wrongly convicted of killing her boss, Helen Stephens thinks she'll surely be cleared soon, except that everyone around her seems to want to keep her in prison. 1___

Dead Ernest - 1982 - Ernest is killed with a champagne cork, then heads off to heaven where the adventure begins. 1___

Dead Pixels - 2019 to present - Three mates spend most of their time playing a role-playing game or thinking about playing a role-playing game. 1___

Dear Green Place - 2007 to 2008 - This Scottish comedy is set in a park in Glasgow, with episodes focusing on various issues in park maintenance. 1___ 2___

Dear John - 1986 to 1987 - A man returns home to find his wife has broken up with him in a note. 1___ 2___

Dear Mother, Love Albert - 1969 to 1972 - An idealistic young northerner heads to London to make his fortune, but falls somewhat short. 1___ 2___ 3___ 4___ | 3 Lost Christmas Specials

Defending the Guilty - 2018 to present - A young barrister learns the ropes from a mentor who hopes to teach him that winning is more important than justice. 1___

Demob - 1993 - After WWII, two soldiers get involved in some questionable deals while trying to adjust to civilian life. 1___

Derek - 2012 to 2014 - Ricky Gervais works as a simple-minded nursing home nurse assistant doing the best he can in spite of the challenges. 1___ 2___

Derry Girls - 2017 to present - This coming-of-age comedy follows the life of a 16-year-old girl and her family during the Troubles. 1___ 2___

Desmond's - 1989 to 1994 - Desmond runs a barber shop, and it becomes a sort of gathering place for odd characters in the neighbourhood. 1___ 2___ 3___ 4___ 5___ 6___

Detectorists - 2014 to 2017 - Two quirky friends scan the fields of England with metal detectors, hoping for the big find that will finally let them do the gold dance. 1___ 2___ 3___ | 2015 Christmas Special___

Dinnerladies - 1998 to 2000 - Comedian Victoria Wood stars in this classic sitcom about workers in a factory canteen. 1___ 2___

Distant Shores - 2005 to 2008 - When a plastic surgeon's veterinarian wife gets a job on a small island, he has to adapt to the lifestyle to hold onto his wife. 1___ 2___

Doc Martin - 2004 to 2019 - After developing a fear of blood and leaving his career as a surgeon, a cantankerous doctor moves to a small Cornish village to practice. 1___ 2___ 3___ 4___ 5___ 6___ 7___ 8___ 9___ | 2001 Movie___

Doctor at the Top - 1991 - This comedy takes a look at the personal and professional lives of doctors. 1___

Don't Drink the Water - 1974 to 1975 - This series was designed as a sequel to On

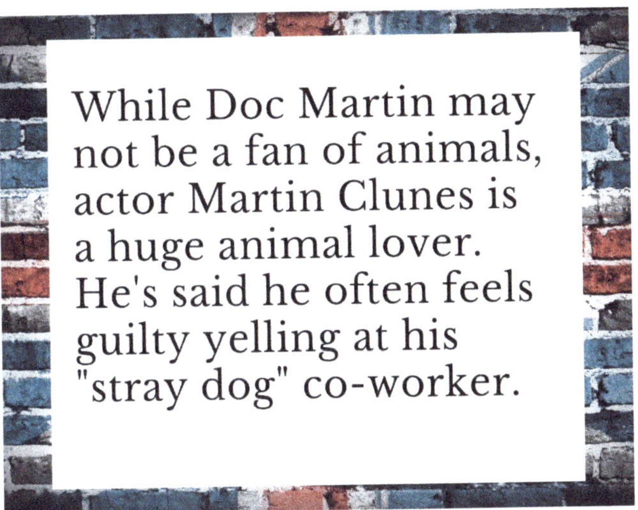

the Buses, and it's set in Spain. 1___ 2___

Don't Forget the Driver - 2019 to present - Toby Jones (*Detectorists*) stars as a coach driver and single father whose life is pretty boring until a dead body shows up along the beach in his small town. 1___

Don't Rock the Boat - 1982 to 1983 - Nigel runs a small yacht building company, and his shrill-voiced daughter and clumsy son-in-law provide comic relief. 1___ 2___

Don't Wait Up - 1983 to 1990 - As a man is getting divorced, his father decides to do the same and move in with him. 1___ 2___ 3___ 4___ 5___ 6___

Down to Earth - 2000 to 2005 - Faith and Brian try to maintain a holiday home in Devon for children who might not otherwise get to see the countryside. 1___ 2___ 3___ 4___ 5___

Dr. Willoughby - 1999 - This series focuses on the cast of a soap opera, both on the set and off it. 1___

Dressing for Breakfast - 1995 to 1998 - A 29-year-old jewelry designer attempts to find "the one" while dealing with interference from her left-wing activist mother. 1___ 2___ 3___

Drifters - 2013 to 2016 - Three young women live quite disastrously in Leeds. 1___ 2___ 3___ 4___

Drop the Dead Donkey - 1990 to 1998 - This classic series looks at a TV news company and the odd characters who work there. 1___ 2___ 3___ 4___ 5___ 6___

Duty Free - 1984 to 1986 - Two couples meet on holiday in Spain, and sparks fly in all the wrong places. 1___ 2___ 3___ | 1986 Christmas Special___

Early Doors - 2003 to 2004 - In Greater Manchester, pub landlord Ken runs his business, worries about his daughter, and tries to get over his wife leaving him for his best friend. 1___ 2___

Edge of Heaven - 2014 - In Margate, a close-knit but quirky family runs a 1980s-themed guest house. 1___

Empty - 2008 - This short-lived Scottish comedy explores what happens when the Greater Glasgow Building Services comes to your home. 1___

Episodes - 2011 to 2018 - Two married TV producers are offered a deal in the US, and then everything goes wrong. 1___ 2___ 3___ 4___ 5___

Ever Decreasing Circles - 1984 to 1989 - An obsessively detail-oriented man drives his wife crazy. Then, a new and more laidback man moves into the neighborhood and catches her eye. 1___ 2___ 3___ 4___ 5___

Executive Stress - 1986 to 1988 - Penelope Keith stars in this sitcom about a couple forced to go undercover to work together, only to have the wife become the husband's boss. 1___ 2___ 3___

Extras - 2005 to 2007 - Ricky Gervais stars as an actor reduced to working as an extra. 1___ 2___

Eyes Down - 2003 to 2004 - This sitcom follows the hardworking staff in a bingo hall. 1___

Faith in the Future - 1995 to 1998 - Faith is enjoying her new single life when her daughter suddenly moves back in with her. 1___ 2___ 3___

Famalam - 2018 to present - This quirky sketch comedy includes bits about everything from Nollywood to "Midsomer F*kn Murders", where a large black 70s NYC cop shows up in a quiet English village.1___ 2___

Father Dear Father - 1968 to 1973 - A single father deals with his two daughters, his agent Georgy, a big St. Bernard called HG, and of course, the nanny. 1___ 2___ 3___ 4___ 5___ 6___ 7___ | 1971 Movie___

Father, Dear Father in Australia - 1978 - When Patrick's brother has an emergency, Patrick and the nanny fly to Australia to look out for his brother's two teen age daughters. 1___

Father Ted - 1995 to 1998 - Father Ted lives with two other very strange priests on the not-so-quiet Craggy Island in Ireland. 1___ 2___ 3___

Fawlty Towers - 1975 to 1979 - John Cleese and Prunella Scales star in this classic British comedy about a very poorly managed hotel. 1___ 2___

Fergus's Wedding - 2002 - *Ireland* - A young Irish couple plans their wedding, but neither of them pass up opportunities for flings. 1___

Ffizz - 1987 to 1989 - Jack and Hugo are wine merchants who drink away their profits and have to find jobs. 1___ 2___

Filthy Rich & Catflap - 1987 - This sitcom was a short-lived satire about a wannabe actor, his agent, and his drunken bodyguard. 1___

First of the Summer Wine - 1988 to 1989 - Set during World War II, First of the Summer Wine was a prequel to Last of the Summer Wine. 1___ 2___

Flat TV - 2016 - Two young men reimagine their boring lives as parodies of various TV shows. 1___

Fleabag - 2016 to present - While trying to come to terms with a tragedy, a young woman makes a mess of her personal life and relationships. 1___ 2___

Flowers - 2016 to present - This dark comedy about an eccentric British family stars Olivia Colman and Julian Barratt. 1___ 2___

For the Love of Ada - 1970 to 1971 - A London widow embarks on a relationship with the Yorkshireman who dug her husband's grave. 1___ 2___ 3___ 4___ | 1972 Movie___

Freezing - 2008 to 2010 - Agent Leon moves into the house with Matt, a British publisher, and Elizabeth, an American actress. 1___

French & Saunders - 1987 to 2017 - Comedy team French and Saunders do sketches about life, TV, and movies. 1___ 2___ 3___ 4___ 5___ 6___ | Christmas Specials: 1988___ 1994___ 2005___ | The Making of the Titantic___ Witless Silence___ The Phantom Millennium___ The Egg___ Celebrity Christmas Puddings___ Actually___

French Fields - 1989 to 1991 - A British couple moves to France and has difficulties adjusting to French culture. 1___ 2___ 3___

Fresh Fields - 1984 to 1986 - A suburban couple must find new hobbies and interests after their children leave the nest. 1___ 2___ 3___ 4___

Fresh Meat - 2011 to 2016 - Six friends prepare to go off to university. 1___ 2___ 3___ 4___

Friday Night Dinner - 2011 to present - Two Jewish brothers always come home to mum and dad's for Friday dinner, and it's never dull. 1___ 2___ 3___ 4___ 5___ | 2012 Christmas Special___

Fried - 2014 to 2015 - This sitcom about a struggling fried chicken shop provides a great example of what not to do when it comes to hiring employees. 1___

Fun at the Funeral Parlour - 2001 to 2002 - This strange series focuses on a Welsh father and his three sons as they run the Thomas, Thomas, Thomas and Thomas funeral parlour together. 1___ 2___

Game On - 1995 to 1998 - Three twentysomething childhood friends from Kent share a flat in London. 1___ 2___ 3___

Gameface - 2017 to present - Roisin Conaty stars as Marcella, a young woman struggling with debt and her love life as she tries to make it as an actress. 1___ 2___

Gap Year - 2017 - This comedy-drama follows a group of young people backpacking through Asia. 1___

Gary: Tank Commander - 2009 to 2012 - This sitcom focuses on the life and antics of a Scottish tank commander and his crew. 1___ 2___ 3___ | 2006 Movie___ 2016 Election Special___

Gates - 2012 - This short-lived sitcom focuses on a couple of parents trying to fit in with the other parents at school. 1___

Gavin & Stacey - 2007 to 2010 - After months of chatting, Gavin and Stacey leave their homes in Essex and Wales to meet for the first time in London. 1___ 2___ 3___ | 2008 Christmas Special___

George & Mildred - 1976 to 1979 - A couple to move to suburbia, where Mildred dreams of upward mobility and George embarrasses her at every turn. 1___ 2___ 3___ 4___ 5___ | 1980 Movie___

Get Back - 1992 to 1993 - This early 90s sitcom about a self-made man fallen on hard times features an early performance from Kate Winslet. 1___ 2___

Get Some In! - 1975 to 1978 - A corporal takes his frustrations out on his men in the 1955 RAF. 1___ 2___ 3___ 4___ 5___

Get Well Soon - 1997 - This hospital comedy takes place at an NHS hospital after the war. 1___

Getting On - 2009 to 2012 - This dark comedy follows the residents and staff in a geriatric ward. 1___ 2___ 3___

Ghosts - 2019 to present - Ghosts attempt to oust the new owners of their crumbling country estate before they can turn it into a hotel. 1___

Gimme Gimme Gimme - 1999 to 2001 - Tom is a gay, unemployed actor with no career, rooming in London with Linda, an unattractive woman who dreams of romance. 1___ 2___ 3___

Going Straight - 1978 - After getting out of prison, a man struggles to be good and stay out of trouble. 1___

Goodbye, Mr. Kent - 1982 - Lazy journalist Travis manipulates his way into a room at Victoria's home. 1___

Grandma's House - 2010 to 2012 - A successful TV presenter quits his job to find more meaningful pursuits, regularly catching up with family at his grandma's house. 1___ 2___

Grandpa in my Pocket - 2009 to 2014 - Thanks to a magical shrinking cap, a boy's grandpa can ride along in his pocket. 1___ 2___ 3___ 4___ 5___

Grange Hill - 1978 to 2008 - This series is all about the lives of the children at the Grange Hill Comprehensive School. 1___ 2___ 3___ 4___ 5___ 6___ 7___ 8___ 9___ 10___ 11___ 12___ 13___ 14___ 15___ 16___ 17___ 18___ 19___ 20___ 21___ 22___ 23___ 24___ 25___ 26___ 27___ 28___ 29___ 30___ 31___

Green Wing - 2004 to 2007 - In this hospital comedy, very few medical things actually happen. 1___ 2___

Grownups - 2006 to 2009 - Young married couples raise their families in Manchester. 1___ 2___ 3___

Hallelujah - 1983 to 1984 - Thora Hird stars as Captain Emily, a woman devoted to charity and determined to flush out sin in rural Yorkshire. 1___ 2___ | 1984 Christmas Special___

Hang Ups - 2018 to present - Stephen Mangan stars as a webcam-based therapist trying to relaunch his practice after professional disaster. 1___

Happy AF - 2019 to present - Aisling Bea stars in this series about a young woman recovering from a breakdown. 1___

Happy Ever After - 1974 to 1978 - Middle aged Terry and June look forward to their empty nest life...until crazy Aunt Lucy and her pet mynah bird move in. 1___ 2___ 3___ 4___ 5___ | Christmas Specials: 1976___ 1977___

Happy Hollidays - 2009 - This Scottish comedy is about life at a fictitious caravan park in Scotland. 1___

Hardware - 2003 to 2004 - Martin Freeman (*Sherlock*) stars in this sitcom

about hardware store workers and their DIY-obsessed customers. 1___ 2___

Harry Enfield & Chums - 1994 to 1999 - This sketch show focuses on the misadventures of oddball and misfit characters. 1___ 2___

Harry Enfield's Television Programme - 1990 to 1992 - This sketch show features more of the comedy of Harry Enfield, including a number of much-loved recurring characters. 1___ 2___

Having it Off - 2002 - This series is set in greater Manchester and features a stereotypically bitchy gay hairdresser whose plans to grow the salon are routinely thwarted by the owner's wife. 1___

Heartburn Hotel - 1998 to 2000 - This odd couple sitcom centers around the owner and occupants of the Olympic Hotel in Birmingham. 1___ 2___

Hebburn - 2012 to 2013 - Set in Hebburn, England, a man brings his new wife home to meet the family, but they don't know he's married. 1___ 2___

Henry IX - 2017 to present - King Henry has a mid-life crisis. 1___

Hi-de-Hi! - 1980 to 1988 - At Maplins, an English holiday camp, the guests are often the last thing on the minds of staff members. 1___ 2___ 3___ 4___ 5___ 6___ 7___ 8___ 9___

High & Dry - 2018 to present - Passengers and crew crash land on a deserted island in the Indian Ocean. 1___

Him & Her - 2010 to 2013 - This sitcom offers a brutally-raw look at a working-class couple of twentysomethings. 1___ 2___ 3___ 4___

Hitmen - 2019 to present - Mel and Sue are two best friends just trying to make their way in the world as professional killers. 1___

Hoff the Record - 2015 to 2016 - In this mockumentary, David Hasselhoff attempts to stage a comeback in the United Kingdom. 1___ 2___

Hold the Sunset - 2018 to 2002 - Two mature neighbors are anxious to start a new life together, but they're interrupted when Edith's adult son arrives on her doorstep. 1___ 2___

Holding the Baby - 1998 - After his wife leaves, high-powered executive Gordon hires a nanny to help him raise his son. 1___

Holding the Fort - 1980 to 1982 - Though commonplace now, this early 80s series was unusual in that it featured a stay-at-home husband with a breadwinner wife. 1___ 2___ 3___

Home - 2017 to present - A new couple goes on holiday to France, and they end up bringing home a most unexpected souvenir. 1___

Home from Home - 2016 to present - A family believes their dream has come true when they buy a home on the lake, until they meet the neighbors. 1___

Home James! - 1987 to 1990 - When Jim loses his job and home, he finds replacements for both as a chauffeur for a businessman. 1___ 2___ 3___ 4___

Home to Roost - 1985 to 1990 - John Thaw stars in this sitcom about a divorcee who's happy with his solitude until his son wants to move in. 1___ 2___ 3___ 4___

Hope it Rains - 1991 to 1992 - After the death of her mother, Jace goes to live with her godfather, the grumpy proprietor of a seaside wax museum. 1___ 2___

House of Fools - 2014 to 2015 - Every episode of this surreal sitcom features uninvited guests in Bob Mortimer's house. 1___ 2___ | 2014 Christmas Special___

How Not to Live Your Life - 2007 to 2011 - Don inherits his grandmother's house, a large mortgage payment, and a strange caretaker. 1___ 2___ 3___ | 2011 Christmas Special___

How to Be a Little Sod - 1995 to 1996 - This series about being a bad baby is told from the baby's perspective. 1___

Hugh & I - 1962 to 1967 - A young bachelor who lives with his mother wants to be rich, but he doesn't want to work for it. 1___ 2___ 3___ 4___ 5___ 6___ | Christmas Specials: 1963___ 1964___

Human Remains - 2000 - Each episode of this black comedy tells the story of a different relationship, documentary-style. 1___

Hunderby - 2012 to 2015 - This sitcom is a black comedy about a woman washed ashore after a shipwreck in the 1830s. 1___ 2___

Hyperdrive - 2006 to 2007 - The crew of a spaceship is sent to encourage alien businesses to relocate to Britain. 1___

I Am Not An Animal - 2004 - This dark comedy features a number of highly intelligent animals who have been rescued from a lab and forced to live on their own. 1___

I Live with Models - 2015 to 2017 - Real life begins for four friends in the fashion industry. 1___

I Want My Wife Back - 2016 - Ben Miller stars as a nice guy who gets blindsided when his wife suddenly leaves him. 1___

I'm Alan Partridge - 1997 to 2002 - Pathetic Alan couldn't hack it as a TV presenter, so he moves to the village of Norwich to do a radio show. 1___ 2___

I'm With Stupid - 2005 to 2006 - When a homeless man needs a place to stay for the night, a wheelchair-bound man helps out and they begin a lasting friendship. 1___

If You See God, Tell Him - 1993 - A man

bumps his head and becomes a devout believer in TV commercials. 1___

Ill Behavior - 2017 to present - After a Hodgkin's lymphoma diagnosis, a man decides to seek natural treatment instead of chemotherapy. His friends are not pleased. 1___

In Loving Memory - 1969 to 1986 - Accident-prone Billy and his Aunt Ivy manage a team at an undertaking firm. 1___ 2___ 3___ 4___ 5___ | 1982 Christmas Special___

In Sickness & in Health - 1985 to 1992 - A couple of pensioners deal with the challenges of aging and the country's social security system. 1___ 2___ 3___ 4___ 5___ 6___ | Christmas Specials: 1985___ 1986___ 1987___ 1989___ 1990___

In with the Flynns - 2011 to 2012 - The Manchester-based Flynn family deals with a fairly standard set of working-class issues. 1___ 2___

Inside No. 9 - 2014 to present - Dark humor, crime, drama, and horror are showcased in this anthology series. 1___ 2___ 3___ 4___ 5___ | 2015 Online-Only Special___ 2018 Halloween Special___

Is It Legal? - 1995 to 1998 - A small law firm somehow manages to survive in spite of overwhelming incompetence. 1___ 2___ 3___

It Ain't Half Hot Mum - 1974 to 1981 - A bunch of misfits form a group to entertain the troops in Burma during WWII. 1___ 2___ 3___ 4___ 5___ 6___ 7___ 8___

IT Crowd - 2006 to 2013 - Competent but odd Moss and Roy work deep in the bowels of a large corporation under their inept boss, Jen. 1___ 2___ 3___ 4___ 5___ | 2013 Special___

It Takes a Worried Man - 1981 to 1983 - A recently divorced man worries about everything. 1___ 2___ 3___

Jack & Dean of All Trades - 2016 to present - Two university friends sign up with a London temp agency that frequently sends them out on strange jobs. 1___ 2___

Jam & Jerusalem aka Clatterford - 2006 to 2009 - This sitcom takes place amongst the members of a women's club. 1___ 2___ 3___ | 2006 Christmas Special___

Jane Hall - 2006 - This early series by writer Sally Wainwright follows the life of Jane Hall as she trains to be a bus driver in London. 1___

Jeeves & Wooster - 1990 to 1993 - Wealthy Wooster gets into trouble and his intelligent butler (Hugh Laurie) gets him out of it. 1___ 2___ 3___ 4___

Joint Account - 1989 to 1990 - Belinda Braithwaite is the primary breadwinner and wants to retire, but her husband David is unwilling to return to the workforce. 1___ 2___

Joking Apart - 1991 to 1995 - A comedian talks about how his marriage went bad. 1___ 2___

Josh - 2014 to present - Three young adults try to get on while a nosy landlord keeps a close eye on them. 1___ 2___ 3___

Judge Romesh - 2018 to present - This unscripted comedy features comedian

Romesh Ranganathan acting as a judge and presiding over actual grievances from the public. 1___

Just a Gigolo - 1993 - Nick is mistaken for a gigolo, but when he loses his job, his brother encourages him to go with it and become one. 1___

Just Good Friends - 1983 to 1986 - 5 years after Vincent leaves Penny at the altar, they meet again and become friends. 1___ 2___ 3___ | 1984 Christmas Special___

Keep it in the Family - 1980 to 1983 - An eccentric comic strip artist is constantly at odds with his agent. 1___ 2___ 3___ 4___ 5___

Keeping Up Appearances - 1990 to 1995 - Dame Patricia Routledge stars as Hyacinth Bucket, a woman in perpetual denial of her working-class roots. 1___ 2___ 3___ 4___ 5___ | Christmas Specials: 1991___ 1993___ 1994___ 1995___ | Children in Need Special___ The Memoirs of Hyacinth Bucket___ Life Lessons from Onslow___ | Young Hyacinth Prequel___

Kiss Me Kate - 1998 to 2001 - A counselor has a partner who is depressed, a neighbor who can't find love, and an Italian who is lovesick over her. 1___ 2___ 3___

In *Keeping Up Appearances*, the "Royal Doulton with the hand-painted periwinkles" is actually a pattern called "Braganza", manufactured by the Colclough China Company (taken over by Royal Doulton)

Knight School - 1997 to 1998 - This children's show is set in the Middle Ages, and takes us to a knight school that decides to take on a scholarship student, a loveable village beggar. 1___ 2___

Lab Rats - 2008 - This sitcom focuses on the lives of staff of a university laboratory. 1___

Ladies of Letters - 2009 to 2010 - Two widows meet under a table at a wedding, then maintain a friendship via letters. 1___ 2___

Last of the Summer Wine - 1973 to 2010 - The world's longest-running sitcom features grandpas gone wild in rural Yorkshire. 1___ 2___ 3___ 4___ 5___ 6___ 7___ 8___ 9___ 10___ 11___12___ 13___ 14___ 15___ 16___ 17___ 18___ 19___ 20___ 21___ 22___ 23___ 24___ 25___ 26___ 27___ 28___ 29___ 30___31___ | Christmas Specials: 1977___ 1978___ 1979___ 1981___ 1982___ 1983___ 1984___ 1986___ 1987___ 1988___ 1989___ 1990___ 1991___ 1992___ 1993___ 1995___ 1996___ 1997___ 2001___ 2002___ 2003___ 2004___ 2005___ 2006___ | New Year's Specials: 1986___ 1995___ 2008___ | Millennium Special___

Law & Disorder - 1994 to 1994 - A female barrister judges the flaws of others but doesn't always hold herself to the same standards. 1___

Lee & Dean - 2018 to present - Two Stevenage-based builders are the best of friends until a woman enters the picture and complicates things. 1___ 2___

Legit - 2006 to 2007 - Two Scottish men sell illegally pirated DVDs and computer games in a Glasgow market. 1___

Life of Riley - 2009 to 2011 - When a newly blended family comes together, dysfunction reigns. Includes Caroline Quentin and Neil Dudgeon. 1___ 2___ 3___

Life's Too Short - 2011 to 2013 - Ricky Gervais stars alongside Warwick Davis, a little person dealing with the frustrations of daily life. 1___

Limmy's Show! - 2009 to 2013 - This Scottish sketch comedy explores a wide variety of dark and bizarre topics. 1___ 2___ 3___ 4___

Linda Green - 2001 to 2002 - This comedy-drama is about the life of a thirtysomething woman who sings by night and sells cars by day. 1___ 2___

Little Britain - 2003 to 2006 - Frequently offensive and always hilarious, this sketch comedy features some of the strangest and most memorable characters to grace British TV screens. 1___ 2___ 3___ 4___ | Little Britain Abroad: 1___ 2___ | Comic Relief Specials: 2007___ 2009___ 2015___ | 2016 Sport Relief Special___

Living the Dream - 2017 to present - When a Yorkshire family buys an RV park in Florida and moves to pursue the American dream, they end up with a serious case of culture shock. 1___ 2___

Lollipop Loves Mr. Mole - 1971 to 1972 - Only a few episodes remain of this opposites-attract couples comedy. 1___ 2___

London Irish - 2013 - Four young Northern Irish ex-pats make their way in London. 1___

Lookalikes - 2015 to present - Part reality show, part comedy, this series explores the difficulties of running a celebrity impersonator agency. 1___ 2___

Los Dos Bros - 2001 - The Dunning Kruger effect is out in full force with these two half-brothers who each think they're handsome, smart, and smooth with the ladies. 1___

Love Thy Neighbour - 1972 to 1976 - When an educated black man moves into a white working-class neighborhood, his neighbor's world is turned upside down. 1___ 2___ 3___ 4___ 5___ 6___ 7___

Lucky Feller - 1975 to 1976 - A shy plumber lives in London with his mother and much cooler brother. 1___

Lunch Monkeys - 2009 to 2011 - The support team for a law firm makes messes, angers their bosses, and maddens their clients as they try to make the best of their unglamourous jobs. 1___ 2___

Maggie & Her - 1976 to 1979 - A divorced schoolteacher lives next door to a nosy neighbour who constantly interferes in her attempts to find love. 1___ 2___

Man About the House - 1973 to 1976 - After a party, two women wake up to find a man in their bathtub. In need of a roommate, they ask him to stay on. 1___ 2___ 3___ 4___ 5___ 6___

Man Down - 2013 to present - Dan is a child trapped in a man's body, and he's not loving adulthood. 1___ 2___ 3___ 4___ | Christmas Specials: 2013___ 2014___

Mann's Best Friends - 1985 - A fussy retired man moves into a boarding house full of strange and unpredictable characters. 1___

Marion & Geoff - 2000 to 2003 - A taxi driver tells the story of his failed marriage after his wife leaves him for a work friend. 1___ 2___

Marley's Ghosts - 2015 to 2016 - After an accident, Marley is haunted by the ghosts of her husband, her lover, and a local vicar. 1___ 2___

Marriage Lines - 1961 to 1966 - This sitcom talks about what really happens in marriages. 1___ 2___ 3___ 4___ 5___

Material Girl - 2010 - A young fashion designer goes up against numerous obstacles to make her way in a cutthroat industry. 1___

Maxxx - 2017 to present - An ex-boy band member turned laughingstock hopes to make a comeback with the help of his ambitious new manager. 1___

May to December - 1989 to 1994 - A widowed Scottish solicitor falls in love with a much younger physical education teacher. 1___ 2___ 3___ 4___ 5___ 6___ | 1990 Christmas Special___

Me & Mrs. Jones - 2012 - Recently divorced Gemma is tempted by her son's friend. Will she be able to resist? 1___

Men Behaving Badly - 1992 to 2014 - Two men in their thirties try to be responsible with the help of their girlfriends. 1___ 2___ 3___ 4___ 5___ 6___ 7___

Mid Morning Matters with Alan Partridge - 2010 to 2016 - DJ Alan talks about how the radio business works. 1___ 2___

Mind Your Language - 1977 to 1986 - A language teacher helps immigrants learn English, but it's not always easy. 1___ 2___ 3___ 4___

Minder - 1979 to 1994 - Dodgy wheeler and dealer Arthur Daley hires former boxer and generally good guy Terry McCann as his bodyguard. 1___ 2___ 3___ 4___ 5___ 6___ 7___ 8___ 9___ 10___

Minder - 2009 - This modern remake of the classic series about a hustler and his good guy bodyguard only lasted one series due to poor reception. 1___

Miranda - 2009 to 2015 - Socially-awkward Miranda runs a joke shop with her best friend and spends much of her time trying not to make a fool of herself. 1___ 2___ 3___ | 2014 Christmas Special___ 2015 New Year's Special___ 2011 Comic Relief___ 2012 Sport Relief___

Misfits - 2009 to 2013 - Misfit offenders develop superpowers when they are struck by lightning. 1___ 2___ 3___ 4___ 5___ | 2010 Christmas Special___

Miss Jones & Son - 1977 to 1978 - A young mother brings her child up alone in London after the journalist father runs out. 1___ 2___

Mister Winner - 2017 to present - A nice bloke with questionable luck must find a job, save for a honeymoon, and hang onto his fiancé. 1___

Mixed Blessings - 1978 to 1980 - A mixed race couple tries to get on while dealing with families that don't approve. 1___ 2___ 3___

Monday Monday - 2009 - This workplace dramedy takes place in the corporate HQ of a grocery company recently forced to relocate. 1___

Monkey Dust - 2003 to 2005 - This darkly satirical animated series covers a variety of controversial topics. 1___ 2___ 3___

Moone Boy - 2012 to 2015 - A young boy's imaginary friend helps him deal with life in a small Irish town. 1___ 2___ 3___

Motherland - 2016 to 2018 - This sitcom explores the dark side of motherhood and parenting in the middle-class world. 1___ 2___

Mount Pleasant - 2011 to present - This light-hearted series follows the day-to-day lives of families in Mount Pleasant. 1___ 2___ 3___ 4___ 5___ 6___ 7___ | 2012 Christmas Special___

Mr. Bean - 1990 to 1995 - Bumbling Mr. Bean rarely speaks and has some very peculiar ways of doing things, but it usually works out for him. 1___ | Bean___ Mr. Bean's Holiday___

Mrs. Brown's Boys - 2011 to present - The matriarch of an Irish family with 6 children loves to meddle in their lives. 1___ 2___ 3___ 4___ | Christmas Specials: 2011___ 2012___ ___ 2013___ ___ 2014___ ___ 2015___ ___ 2016___ ___ 2017___ ___ | 2016 Live Special___

Mrs. Thursday - 1966 to 1967 - Kindly housekeeper Mrs. Thursday gets everything when her boss dies. 1___ 2___ 3___

Mulberry - 1992 to 1993 - The son of Death and Springtime is supposed to start his job as the Grim Reaper by collecting Miss Fanaby, but doesn't get the job done. 1___ 2___

Mum - 2016 to present - After her husband dies, a woman tries to rebuild her life amidst all manner of problems from family and friends. 1___ 2___ 3___

Mumbai Calling - 2007 to 2008 - A British-born Indian man is sent to take over operations at a Mumbai call center because management thinks he'll be able to identify with the workers. 1___

Murder Most Horrid - 1991 to 1999 - Dawn French stars in this dark comedy anthology that pokes fun at the conventions of the old horror and thriller anthology shows. 1___ 2___ 3___ 4___

Mutual Friends - 2008 - Martin and Patrick come together when Martin's best friend takes his own life. 1___

My Family - 2000 to 2011 - A grumpy dentist and his busy wife struggle to find enough time and energy for each other and their children. 1___ 2___ 3___ 4___ 5___ 6___ 7___ 8___ 9___ 10___ 11___ | Christmas Specials: 2002___ 2003___ 2004___ 2005___ 2006___ 2007___ 2008___ 2009___ 2010___

My Good Friend - 1995 to 1996 - Two lonely old pensioners meet a single mother and her son, forming a relationship that works for all of them. 1___ 2___

MY NOTES

My Hero - 2000 to 2007 - A superhero from planet Ultron tries to blend into human life as George Sunday. 1___ 2___ 3___ 4___ 5___ 6___

My Mad Fat Diary - 2013 to 2015 - In 1996 Lincolnshire, a young girl attempts to readjust to life after getting out of a psychiatric facility. 1___ 2___ 3___

My Old Man - 1974 to 1975 - An opinionated old Yorkshireman lives under the same roof as his daughter and son-in-law. 1___ 2___

My Wife Next Door - 1972 to 1973 - When George and Suzie divorce, they both move to the country and find themselves living next door to one another. 1___

Nathan Barley - 2005 - After publishing a rant about idiot scenesters, a man is horrified to find himself the object of their admiration. 1___

Nearest & Dearest - 1968 to 1973 - Sister and brother Eli and Nellie take over the family business after the death of their father. Eli doesn't want to focus on the business. 1___ 2___ 3___ 4___ 5___ 6___ 7___

Never Say Die - 1987 - A single mother is appointed as warden in a housing block full of hard-to-control elderly residents. 1___

Nighty Night - 2004 to 2005 - This black comedy focuses on a narcissistic sociopath and the horrible things she does to manipulate the people around her. 1___ 2___

No Angels - 2004 to 2006 - This sitcom shows us what nurses get up to in their off-hours. 1___ 2___ 3___

No Heroics - 2008 to 2009 - Superheroes exist in modern-day London, but they still have to do their shopping and laundry like the rest of us. 1___

No Job for a Lady - 1990 to 1992 - Penelope Keith stars in this comedy about a suburban woman and newly-elected MP for the left-wing Labour Party. 1___ 2___ 3___

No Place Like Home - 1983 to 1988 - Arthur and Beryl were looking forward to their empty nest years, but it's not meant to be in this comedy. A very young Martin Clunes makes an appearance. 1___ 2___ 3___ 4___ 5___

No, Honestly - 1974 to 1975 - C.D. and Clara tell stories about how they met and fell in love. 1___

No, That's Me Over Here - 1967 to 1970 - Ronnie Corbett struggles in the midst of suburban status races. 1___ 2___ 3___

Nobody's House - 1978 - The ghost of a young boy haunts a family's new home. 1___

Northern Lights - 2006 - Robson Green and Mark Benton are best friends with an intense rivalry. 1___

Not Going Out - 2006 to present - This comedy showcases the misadventures of Lee, a young slacker in a mysteriously spacious London flat. 1___ 2___ 3___ 4___ 5___ 6___ 7___ 8___ 9___ | Christmas Specials: 2013___ 2015___ 2017___ | 2012 Children in Need Special___

Not in Front of the Children - 1967 to 1970 - Only 8 episodes remain of this series about a scatter-brained young mother. 1___

2___ 3___ 4___

Not on Your Nellie - 1974 to 1975 - A spinster inherits a shabby London pub and decides to give running it a go. 1___ 2___ 3___

Not the Nine O'Clock News - 1979 to 1982 - This sketch news comedy features Mel Smith and Rowan Atkinson. 1___ 2___ 3___ 4___

Not with a Bang - 1990 - After a lab accident, only four people are left on earth. 1___

Nurse - 2015 - This sitcom follows a psychiatric nurse, her patients, and her coworkers in a small community. 1___

Off the Hook - 2009 - Danny is ready for a fresh start at university, but an old mate shows up to ruin those plans. 1___

Oh Brother! - 1968 to 1970 - A new monk has good intentions, but his frequent mishaps frustrate the monastery leaders. 1___ 2___ 3___

Oh Father! - 1973 - In this follow-up to *Oh Brother!*, Derek Nimmo plays a clumsy and awkward monk recently promoted from Brother to Father. 1___

Oh No It's Selwyn Froggit - 1974 to 1977 - A lovable buffoon livens up a sleepy Yorkshire village. 1___ 2___ 3___

Oh, Doctor Beeching! - 1995 to 1997 - Dr. Beeching was a man whose study of the British railways was used to make sweeping cuts around the country. This series takes place at a small branch line station threatened by those cuts. 1___ 2___

On the Buses - 1969 to 1973 - A bus driver and his coworkers are more interested in women than doing their jobs. 1___ 2___ 3___ 4___ 5___ 6___ 7___

On the Up - 1990 to 1992 - A self-made millionaire seems to be surrounded by people who make his life harder. 1___ 2___ 3___

Only Fools & Horses - 1981 to 2003 - This comedy follows a couple of dodgy brothers always out for the big score. 1___ 2___ 3___ 4___ 5___ 6___ 7___ | Christmas Specials: 1981___ 1982___ 1983___ 1985___ 1986___ 1987___ 1988___ 1989___ 1990___ 1991___ ___ 1992___ 1993___ 1996___ ___ ___ 2001___ 2002___ 2003___

Only When I Laugh - 1979 to 1982 - Three patients cause headaches for hospital staff. 1___ 2___ 3___ 4___

Open All Hours - 1973 to 1985 - A tightwad shopkeeper works hard alongside his long-suffering nephew in this classic British sitcom. 1___ 2___ 3___ 4___ | 1982 Christmas Special___

Oscar's Hotel for Fantastical Creatures - 2015 - When Oscar leaves town, he appoints his nephew to manage his hotel full of strange creatures. 1___

Our Ex-Wife - 2016 - Jack's unhinged ex-wife Hillary is determined to destroy his newfound happiness. 1___

Outnumbered - 2007 to 2014 - This semi-improvised comedy explores the harsh and occasionally hilarious reality of being outnumbered by your children. 1___ 2___

3__ 4__ 5__ | Christmas Specials: 2009__ 2011__ 2012__ 2016__

Outside Edge - 1994 to 1996 - Brenda Blethyn stars in this comedy about two couples who run a local cricket team and see things very differently. 1__ 2__ 3__

Pardon the Expression - 1965 to 1966 - This *Coronation Street* spinoff sees Mr. Swindley acting as deputy manager at the Dobson and Hawks department store. 1__ 2__

Parents - 2012 - A businesswoman finds out her husband has lost their life savings on the day she loses her job, and they have to go live with her parents. 1__

Paris - 1994 - This series features the escapades of a French artist (with an English accent) trying to get famous in 1920s Paris. 1__

Peep Show - 2003 to 2015 - Mark and Jez are flatmates and complete opposites who constantly manage to find trouble. 1__ 2__ 3__ 4__ 5__ 6__ 7__ 8__ 9__

In *Only Fools & Horses...*, outdoor scenes were actually filmed in Bristol because the insurance to film in Peckham would have been too expensive.

People Just Do Nothing - 2014 to present - This mockumentary follows a group of bad wannabe MCs from West London. 1__ 2__ 3__ 4__ 5__

Perfect Scoundrels - 1990 to 1992 - Two con-men travel around and defraud people. 1__ 2__ 3__

Peter Kay's Car Share - 2015 to 2018 - Two grocery store employees participate in their company's car-share scheme, and each episode takes place during their commute. 1__ 2__ | 2016 Christmas Comedy Shuffle__ Unscripted__ The Finale__

PhoneShop - 2009 to 2013 - This sitcom follows the lives of misfit employees at a phone store. 1__ 2__ 3__

Playing the Field - 1998 to 2002 - A poorly-managed female football team out of South Yorkshire has very little chance of winning anything, but they do try. 1__ 2__ 3__ 4__ 5__

Plaza Patrol - 1991 - Two men work as highly incompetent mall security guards. 1__

Please Sir! - 1968 to 1972 - While the other teachers at his school have lost hope, a hapless and kind-hearted teacher sees the good in his students. 1__ 2__ 3__ 4__ | 1971 Film__

Plebs - 2013 to present - Three young men make their way in Ancient Rome. 1__ 2__ 3__ 4__ 5__

Pompidou - 2015 - Having fallen on hard times, an aristocrat is forced to live in a camper with his butler and his dog. 1___

Porkpie - 1995 to 1996 - A struggling lollipop man (crossing guard) borrows a pound to buy a lottery ticket and wins. 1___

Porridge - 1973 to 1977 - This prison comedy features a man trying to do his time honestly and stay out of trouble. 1___ 2___ 3___

Porters - 2017 to present - When an enthusiastic hospital porter shows up for his first day at work, his fellow porters give him a rude awakening. 1___ 2___

Pramface - 2012 to 2014 - A young woman near Edinburgh sleeps with a younger boy at a party and gets pregnant. 1___ 2___ 3___

Psychoville - 2009 to 2011 - When a bunch of strangers receive the same note, their lives begin to fall apart. 1___ 2___

Pulling - 2006 to 2009 - While celebrating her hen night, Donna realizes she's missed out on the single life and calls off her wedding. 1___ 2___ 3___

Punchdrunk - 1993 - This Glasgow-based boxing comedy didn't last long, but it did feature Diana Hardcastle (*Best Exotic Marigold Hotel*) in an early role. 1___

Puppy Love - 2014 - Two women share a friendship as they cope with rowdy dogs, difficult teenagers, and imperfect husbands. 1___

Pure - 2019 to present - 24-year-old Marnie suffers from a form of OCD nicknamed "Pure O" for the focused sexual thoughts it causes. 1___

Quacks - 2017 - This zany and occasionally absurdist comedy follows four doctors in Victorian London. 1___

Rab C. Nesbitt - 1988 to 2014 - A "proud of it" lowlife talks to the camera about life as he sees it from his drunken perspective in Glasgow. 1___ 2___ 3___ 4___ 5___ 6___ 7___ 8___ 9___ 10___ | Christmas Specials: 1988___ 2008___ | 1992 Live Special___ 2014 New Year's Special___

Raffles - 1975 to 1977 - Raffles is a celebrity cricket player and an expert jewel thief. 1___ 2___

Raised by Wolves - 2013 to 2016 - A single mother raises her large family in a not-so-conventional way. 1___ 2___

Red Dwarf - 1988 to present - In the far future, the last human lives aboard a spaceship with a highly evolved cat-man. 1___ 2___ 3___ 4___ 5___ 6___ 7___ 8___ 9___ 10___11___12___13___

Reggie Perrin - 2009 to 2010 - Martin Clunes stars in this remake of the classic Reginald Perrin stories. 1___ 2___

Relative Strangers - 1985 to 1987 - A cocky teenage son comes to live with his estranged father. 1___ 2___

Rev - 2010 to 2014 - This sitcom follows the adventures of an Anglican vicar, his wife, and his run-down inner-city parish. 1___ 2___ 3___

Rising Damp - 1974 to 1978 - Tenants show up their nasty landlord in different ways. 1___ 2___ 3___ 4___

Robin's Nest - 1977 to 1981 - Robin is a chef

with a girlfriend and business in this spinoff of Man About the House. 1___ 2___ 3___ 4___ 5___ 6___ | Christmas Specials: 1979___ 1980___

Rock & Chips - 2010 to 2011 - This spinoff of *Only Fools and Horses* serves as a prequel about Del Boy's teenage years. 1___

Roger Roger - 1996 to 2003 - This dramedy revolves around a mini-cab firm in London.

Roll Over Beethoven - 1985 - A heavy metal musician falls for a classical music teacher in an English village. 1___ 2___ 3___

Romany Jones - 1972 to 1975 - A sweet young couple move into a caravan site next door to a disgusting old couple. 1___ 2___ 3___4___

Room at the Bottom - 1986 to 1988 - A failed drama producer is demoted to the quiz show department. 1___ 2___

Room Service - 1979 - Hotel staff members manage to get into all sorts of trouble. 1___

Round Planet - 2016 - Matt Lucas stars as nature documentarian Armstrong Wedgewood in this parody of nature programs. 1___

Sally4Ever - 2018 to present - After 10 boring, suburban years, David asks Sally to marry him and she embarks on a fling with a woman. 1___

Sando - 2018 to present - *Australia* - Sando is the queen of package furniture deals in Australia. 1___

Saxondale - 2006 to 2007 - An ex-roadie with anger management issues shares his wisdom with the innocent assistant who helps in his pest control business. 1___ 2___

School Bus - 2019 to present - This sitcom focuses on 12-year-old Noah Beckett and his daily time on the school bus. 1___

Scot Squad - 2014 to present - This mockumentary follows Glasgow police officers as they encounter a variety of interesting scenarios. 1___ 2___ 3___ 4___

Screaming - 1992 - A group of women share friendship and a man. 1___

Scrotal Recall aka Lovesick - 2014 to present - After finding out he has an STD, a young man must attempt to contact former lovers to inform them of their possible fates. 1___ 2___ 3___

Sean's Show - 1992 to 1993 - Comedian Sean Hughes stars in a sitcom about himself, aware that he's in a sitcom. 1___ 2___

Second Thoughts - 1991 to 1994 - Middle-aged divorcees want to enter a relationship, but get resistance from the people around them. 1___ 2___ 3___ 4___ 5___

Sensitive Skin - 2005 to 2007 - Joanna Lumley (*Absolutely Fabulous*) stars in this story of a mature woman and how she handles the problems in her life. 1___ 2___

Shameless - 2004 to 2013 - The shameless Gallagher family lives, loves, and gets into trouble on a rundown Manchester housing estate. 1___ 2___ 3___ 4___ 5___ 6___ 7___ 8___ 9___ 10___11___

Shane - 2017 to present - Shane introduces funny and interesting YouTube content. 1___

2___ 3___

Shelley - 1979 to 1984 - An educated neer-do-well and professional bum battles almost everyone in his life. 1___ 2___ 3___ 4___ 5___ 6___

Shillingbury Tales - 1980 to 1981 - Londoners move to the countryside and meet loads of eccentric locals. 1___

Shine on Harvey Moon - 1982 to 1995 - A man returns home from WWII to find his wife uninterested in their marriage, so he busies himself with local politics. 1___ 2___ 3___ 4___ 5___

Siblings - 2014 to 2016 - Hannah and her younger brother Dan share a flat in London and bring about all manner of chaos with their selfish, carefree ways. 1___ 2___

Sick Note - 2017 to present - When a man is believed to be fatally ill, he finds that people are nicer to him. When he finds out the truth, he thinks he may continue the pretense. 1___ 2___

Sick of It - 2018 to present - Karl is a bored taxi driver who lives with his elderly aunt and deals with an outspoken inner voice. 1___

Sink or Swim - 1980 to 1982 - Brian's life is already messy, then his lazy brother comes to London and makes things worse. 1___ 2___ 3___

Sitting Pretty - 1992 to 1993 - When a woman's wealthy husband dies and leaves her penniless, she moves back in with her rural family. 1___ 2___

Slinger's Day - 1986 to 1987 - A London supermarket manager deals with an inept staff. This series is a continuation of *Tripper's Day* after the death of its lead. 1___ 2___

Smith & Jones - 1989 to 1998 - In this follow-up to *Alas Smith and Jones*, the duo continues to perform short sketches about modern life, many of which are in poor taste. 1___ 2___ 3___ 4___ 5___ 6___

Snakes & Ladders - 1989 to present - Set in the "future" of 1999, a noble decides his son needs real life experience in the cold and impoverished north, while a poor man is sent down to luxurious southern England in his place. 1___

Snuff Box - 2006 - Two hangmen are competitive, constantly trying to outdo each other when it comes to matters of women and money. 1___

So Awkward - 2015 to 2017 - This Manchester-based series follows three socially awkward teenage girls. 1___ 2___ 3___

So Haunt Me - 1992 to 1994 - When a family moves into their new home, they find the ghost of a Jewish woman still occupies it. 1__ 2__ 3__

So You Think You've Got Troubles - 1991 to present - A secular Jew is transferred to work in heavily Christian and Catholic Belfast. 1__

Soft Border Patrol - 2018 to present - In this satirical comedy, a border agency keeps track of those who wander the border between the EU and the UK. 1__

Some Girls - 2012 to 2014 - Four South London schoolgirls deal with life, love, and growing up. 1__ 2__ 3__

Some Mothers Do 'Ave Em - 1973 to 1978 - Accident-prone Frank can't seem to do anything right, aside from marrying a very tolerant woman. 1__ 2__ 3__ | Christmas specials: 1974__ 1975__ 1978__ | 2016 Sport Relief Sketch__

Sorry - I'm a Stranger Here Myself - 1981 to 1982 - Henpecked librarian Henry leaves his wife to go live in his childhood home, only to find it occupied by a punk squatter and surrounded by neighbours who don't like him. 1__ 2__

Sorry! - 1981 to 1988 - A 41 year old man's mother prevents him from leaving home. 1__ 2__ 3__ 4__ 5__ 6__ 7__

Spaced - 1999 to 2001 - North Londoners Tim and Daisy pretend to be a couple so they can afford an apartment. 1__ 2__

Spitting Image - 1984 to 1996 - Major public figures are turned into puppets to satirize British life. 1__ 2__ 3__ 4__ 5__ 6__ 7__ 8__ 9__ 10__ 11__ 12__13__ 14__ 15__ 16__ 17__ 18__ 19__ | Down And Out In The White House__ The Spitting Image 1987 Movie Awards__ 1987 Election Special__ A Non-Denominational Spitting Image Holiday Special__ The Ronnie And Nancy Show__ Bumbledown - The Life and Times of Ronald Reagan__ The Sound Of Maggie__ 1992 Election Special__ The Spitting Image Pantomime__ Ye Olde Spitting Image__ Spitting Image at 30__

Spooner's Patch - 1979 to 1982 - This sitcom revolves around the general incompetence and corruption of a small suburban police department. 1__ 2__ 3__

Spring & Autumn - 1972 to 1976 - After his home is demolished, an old railway worker goes to live in a high-rise with his daughter, eventually befriending a 12-year-old boy. 1__ 2__ 3__ 4__

Spy - 2011 to 2012 - Tim thinks he's applying for a civil servant job, but he's offered a position as a spy trainee instead. 1__ 2__

Starting Out - 1999 - A young girl is engaged to a boring businessman, but falls in love with an exciting footballer. 1__

Stath Lets Flats - 2018 to present - Lettings agent Stath works in North London with his Greek father and tries to prove himself worthy of the family business. 1__

Steptoe & Son - 1962 to 1974 - This classic British comedy centers around a father and son who are rag-and-bone men (junk collectors). 1__ 2__ 3__ 4__ 5__ 6__ 7__ 8__ | Christmas Specials: 1973__ 1974__

Still Game - 2002 to present - Still Game is a quirky Scottish comedy about three old men in a Glasgow high-rise. 1___ 2___ 3___ 4___ 5___ 6___ 7___ 8___ 9___ | Christmas Specials: 2005___ 2007___ Hogmanay Specials: 2006___ 2007___ | Live at the Hydro___ Children in Need Special___ The Story So Far___

Still Open All Hours - 2013 to present - After inheriting his uncle's shop, Granville continues to run it as it's always been run. 1___ 2___ 3___ 4___ 5___ | 2013 Christmas Special___

Sunshine - 2008 - Mr. Bing wants to do right, but his penchant for gambling always ruins things. M___

SunTrap - 2015 - When reporter Woody is framed by his boss, he hides out with an old journalist mentor on a Spanish Island. 1___

Surgical Spirit - 1989 to 1995 - Although Sheila is a great surgeon, she sometimes has trouble navigating the hospital's "old boys network". 1___ 2___ 3___ 4___ 5___ 6___ 7___

Sykes - 1972 to 1979 - Twins take pleasure in annoying their snooty neighbor. 1___ 2___ 3___ 4___ 5___ 6___ 7___ | 1977 Christmas Special___

Take a Letter Mr. Jones - 1981 - This sitcom features a high-powered female executive fighting her way to the top with largely inept support staff. 1___

Takin' Over the Asylum - 1994 - An employee in a mental hospital starts a radio station within the facility. 1___

Tears Before Bedtime - 1995 - A middle-class British family wrestles with ways to achieve domestic harmony. 1___

Telford's Change - 1979 - Though Telford has achieved great success in his banking career, he takes a step backwards to become a local branch manager in Dover. 1___

Terri McIntyre - 2003 to 2004 - This Scottish comedy stars Simon Carlyle as the cross-dressing Terri McIntyre, owner of a Glasgow tanning salon. Series 2 includes David Tennant. 1___ 2___

Terry & June - 1979 to 1987 - This sequel to *Happy Ever After* features the same couple and basic premise (empty nesters going about their lives), but it dropped Aunt Lucy and the mynah bird. 1___ 2___ 3___ 4___ 5___ 6___ 7___ 8___ 9___ | Christmas specials: 1980___ 1981___ 1982___ 1985___

The Army Game - 1957 to 1961 - This sitcom features a group of conscripts trying to do as little as possible in the post-war British army. 1___ 2___ 3___ 4___ 5___

The Bleak Old Shop of Stuff - 2011 to 2012 - This show parodies the works of Charles Dickens. 1___

The Book Group - 2002 to 2003 - When an American woman moves to Glasgow, she starts a book group to help get to know people. 1___ 2___

The Bounder - 1982 to 1983 - After a prison stay, ex-con Howard moves in with his sister and brother-in-law and uses his criminal skills to get by. 1___ 2___

The Brighton Belles - 1993 to 1994 - This British remake of *The Golden Girls*

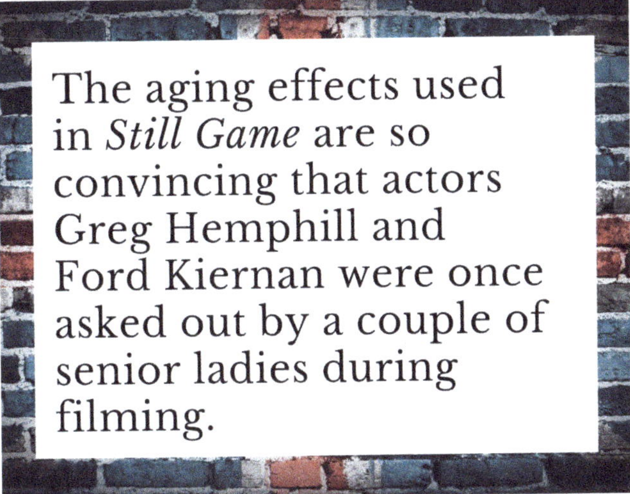

performed so poorly that it was pulled halfway through its run. 1___ 2___

The Brittas Empire - 1991 to 1997 - Despite good intentions and ambition, Gordon's efforts at work often go astray. 1___ 2___ 3___ 4___ 5___ 6___ 7___ | Christmas Specials: 1994___ 1996___

The Cafe - 2011 to 2013 - This sitcom revolves around a trio of women running a cafe in the seaside town of Weston-super-Mare. 1___ 2___

The Champions - 1968 to 1969 - International Intelligence agents crash into a lost civilization and come away with superpowers. 1___

The Chase - 2006 to 2007 - A veterinarian gets married and turns his practice over to his two very different daughters. 1___ 2___

The Complete Guide to Parenting - 2006 - When his wife moves to Paris for a job, a child psychology professor has to draw on all his book learning to take care of his 7-year-old son. 1___

The Cuckoo Waltz - 1975 to 1980 - Newlyweds in financial trouble rent out their room to a lodger. 1___ 2___ 3___ 4___

The Delivery Man - 2015 - Matthew Bunting is a former police officer turned male midwife. 1___

The Detectives - 1993 to 1997 - Two detective constables have plenty of hunches, most of them wrong. 1___ 2___ 3___ 4___ 5___ | Christmas Specials: 1995___ 1997___

The Dustbinmen - 1969 to 1970 - This sitcom focuses on the men who collect dustbins. 1___ 2___ 3___

The End of the F*ing World** - 2017 to present - In this strange dark comedy, a teenage psychopath embarks on a road trip with the intention of killing his rebel companion. 1___ 2___

The Estate Agents - 2000 to 2002 - This short-lived sitcom focuses on the personal and professional lives of estate agents. 1___

The Fall & Rise of Reginald Perrin - 1976 to 1979 - After a mid-life crisis, a man fakes his own death and later returns to his old job in disguise. 1___ 2___ 3___ | 1982 Christmas Sketch___

The Fitz - 2000 - This sitcom features a rowdy Irish family living on the border of Ireland and Northern Ireland. 1___

The Gaffer - 1981 to 1983 - This early 80s sitcom features Bill Maynard as a struggling small business owner. 1___ 2___ 3___

The Gemma Factor - 2009 to 2010 - Realistic characters show how the entertainment industry can be subversive and opportunistic. 1___

The Good Guys - 1992 to 1993 - Nigel Havers and Keith Barron star in this comedy-drama about an unlikely couple of friends. 1___ 2___

The Good Life aka Good Neighbors - 1975 to 1978 - A man wakes up on his 40th birthday and decides to quit the rat race, turning his suburban home into a self-sufficient farm with his wife. 1___ 2___ 3___ 4___ | 1977 Christmas Special___ 1978 Royal Command Performance___

The Goodies - 1970 to 1982 - A three-man British comedy group does pretty much any kind of comedy, anytime they like. 1___ 2___ 3___ 4___ 5___ 6___ 7___ 8___ 9___ | Kitten Kong: Montreux '72 Edition___ A Collection of Goodies - Special Tax Edition___

The Gravy Train - 1990 - An idealistic young man gets involved in politics and encounters all the things you would expect in politics. 1___

The Gravy Train Goes East - 1991 - A liberated female politician wants her country to join the EU, but has to work with the idealistic Hans Dorfman. M___

The Great Outdoors - 2010 - Ruth Jones (*Gavin & Stacey*) and Katherine Parkinson (*Doc Martin*) star in this sitcom about the eccentric members of a rambling club. 1___

The Green Green Grass - 2005 to 2009 - A sleazy car salesman and his family move from London to a country farmhouse. 1___ 2___ 3___ 4___

The High Life - 1994 to 1995 - Alan Cumming stars in this Scottish sitcom about life in the fictitious Prestwick Airport. 1___

The History of Mr. Polly - 1980 - This miniseries is based on the HG Wells comic novel by the same name, and it tells the story of a bumbling man for whom things usually work out. M___

The Inbetweeners - 2008 to 2010 - This clever but bawdy teenage comedy follows four friends as they navigate their final years of school and entrance into adulthood. 1___ 2___ 3___ | 2011 Movie___ 2014 Movie___

The Job Lot - 2013 to 2015 - In a Midlands job centre, it's hard to tell if anyone actually works. 1___ 2___ 3___

The Kennedys - 2015 - In this 1970s period comedy, a family moves to a new community where they can be seen as middle-class. 1___

The Kit Curran Radio Show - 1984 - An obnoxious and self-obsessed DJ refuses to follow the rules. 1___

The Kumars - 2014 - This revival of *The Kumars at No. 42* features a new living arrangement. 1___

The Kumars at No. 42 - 2001 to 2006 - Kumar is a talk show host who interviews guests in his home, but his family gets in the way. 1___ 2___ 3___ 4___ 5___ 6___ 7___

The Labours of Erica - 1989 to 1990 - When she finds a childhood list of goals,

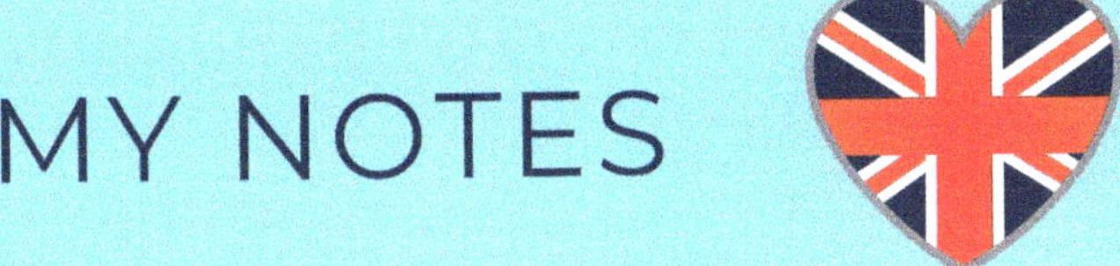
MY NOTES

Erica (Brenda Blethyn, *Vera*) resolves to complete them all by the age of 40. 1__ 2__

The Larkins - 1958 to 1964 - Alf Larkins is a henpecked man who won't admit it. 1__ 2__ 3__ 4__ 5__ 6__ | Inn for Trouble__

The Last Laugh - 2005 to 2006 - Established sitcom writers create new programs, and new writers have to come up with the endings. 1__

The League of Gentlemen - 1999 to 2017 - In the fictional Northern England town of Royston Vasey, strange characters exist with interweaving storylines. 1__ 2__ 3__ | 2000 Christmas Special__ 2017 Anniversary Special__

The Legacy of Reginald Perrin - 1996 - This follow-up to *The Fall & Rise of Reginald Perrin* shows a fortune left to family and friends with strange conditions. 1__

The Life & Times of Vivian Vyle - 2007 - Jennifer Saunders stars as a daytime TV presenter and agony aunt. 1__

The Likely Lads - 1964 to 1966 - This sitcom follows the story of two lads, one who tries to be responsible and another who's decidedly less so. 1__ 2__ 3__

The Liver Birds - 1969 to 1996 - Set in Liverpool in the days after Beatlemania, two young unmarried women share a flat and enjoy their newfound independence. 1__ 2__ 3__ 4__ 5__ 6__ 7__ 8__ 9__ 10__ | Christmas Night with the Stars__ Christmas Specials: 1975__ 1976__ 1977__

The Lovers - 1970 to 1971 - This early 70s sitcom focuses on two young people falling in love. 1__ 2__

The Management - 1988 - Comedians Hall & Pace star as a couple of guys who inherit a nightclub and manage it terribly. 1__

The Midnight Beast - 2012 to 2014 - Three boys start a band and try to get famous. 1__ 2__

The Mighty Boosh - 2003 to 2007 - Vince and Howard try to make a living as musicians while also working at a zoo with madman Bob. 1__ 2__ 3__

The New Statesman - 1987 to 1992 - This parody of 1980s Conservatism follows a Machiavellian Tory. 1__ 2__ 3__ 4__ | 1988 Comic Relief__ Who Shot Alan B'Stard__ A B'Stard Exposed__

The Office - 2001 to 2003 - Ricky Gervais and Mackenzie Crook appear in this sitcom that inspired the US version of *The Office*. 1__ 2__ | 2003 Christmas Special__ __ | The Office Revisited__

The Old Guys - 2009 to 2010 - Two old guys live together, and both have a thing for the attractive woman who lives next door. 1__ 2__

The Other 'Arf - 1980 to 1984 - A rich politician falls in love with a model from the working class. 1__ 2__ 3__ 4__

The Other One - 2017 to present - Two sisters, each called Catherine Walcott, have no idea the other exists until their shared father drops dead. 1__

The Peter Principle aka The Boss -

1995 to 2000 - Bumbling bank manager Peter is hopelessly inept and constantly in fear of his assistant manager, who actually seems to be running the place. 1___ 2___

The Piglet Files - 1990 to 1992 - Electronics Professor Peter becomes a reluctant MI-5 agent and tries to keep it a secret from his wife. 1___ 2___ 3___

The Professionals - 1977 to 1983 - Top CI5 agents fight terrorism and other high-profile crimes. 1___ 2___ 3___ 4___ 5___

The Rag Trade - 1961 to 1963 - In a women's clothing factory, the staff of female machinists like to give the foreman a hard time. 1___ 2___ 3___

The Rebel - 2016 to 2017 - A grumpy retired man rebels against everything, leaving his friends and family to clean up whatever messes he makes. 1___ 2___

The Reluctant Landlord - 2018 to present - Romesh Ranganathan stars as a man left running the local pub after his father leaves it to him in his will and his family pressures him to stay. 1___

The Robinsons - 2005 - Martin Freeman plays the role of an actuary who decides to reimagine his life after realizing he doesn't enjoy his work. 1___

The Royal Bodyguard - 2011 to 2012 - A retired soldier is brought in to take charge of royal security, but he's not very good at it. 1___

The Royle Family - 1998 to 2012 - This sitcom features a scruffy, argumentative, telly-obsessed family in Manchester. 1___ 2___ 3___ 4___ | Christmas Specials: 1999___ 2000___ 2008___ 2009___ 2010___ 2012___ | 2006 Queen of Sheba___ | 2008 Children in Need___ 2009 Comic Relief___

The Spa - 2013 - Strange things happen in a Hertfordshire health spa. 1___

The Squirrels - 1974 to 1976 - Employees of International Rentals spend most of their time covering up their mistakes and avoiding actual work. 1___ 2___ 3___

The Steamie - 1988 - This dramedy is about 1950s Glasgow women who wash their clothing at the same washhouse. 1___

The Sweeney - 1975 to 1978 - Rough-around-the-edges detective Jack Regan works in London and often uses tactics as illegal as the crimes he's trying to fight. 1___ 2___ 3___ 4___

The Thick of It - 2005 to 2012 - This political satire follows government officials who lie, cheat, and generally do whatever it takes to keep their jobs. 1___ 2___ 3___ 4___ | 2007 Specials: Rise of the Nutters___ Spinners and Losers___ |

The Top Secret Life of Edgar Briggs - 1974 - A clueless assistant to the British Intelligence Service Commander somehow manages to solve cases. 1___

The Trip - 2010 to 2017 - Steve Coogan and Rob Brydon star in this sitcom about a restaurant reviewer and his tagalong friend who ends up helping out more than planned. 1___ 2___ 3___

The Two of Us - 1986 to 1990 - Nicholas Lyndhurst stars in this series about a young couple living in a basement apartment. 1__ 2__ 3__ 4__ | 1988 Christmas Special__

The Two Ronnies - 1971 to 1987 - Comedians Ronnie Barker and Ronnie Corbett present humorous sketches and musical routines. 1__ 2__ 3__ 4__ 5__ 6__ 7__ 8__ 9__ 10__ 11__ 12__

The Upchat Collection - 1978 - Mike Upchat lives out of a left luggage locker in Marylebone Station and spends most of his time trying to sponge off friends or woo beautiful women. 1__ 2__

The Upper Hand - 1990 to 1996 - A male housekeeper comes to the aid of an affluent divorced mother raising her son. 1__ 2__ 3__ 4__ 5__ 6__ 7__

The Vital Spark - 1965 to 1975 - Though most episodes of this Scottish tugboat comedy have been lost, a handful have been released on DVD. 1__ 2__ 3__

The Wackers - 1975 - After two years in prison, a man rejoins his family in Liverpool, trying hard to readjust. 1__

The Windsors - 2016 to present - This mockumentary parodies the current British royal family. 1__ 2__ | 2018 Royal Wedding Special__

The World According to Smith & Jones - 1987 to 1988 - This Smith and Jones production featured more sketches, and came in between *Alas Smith & Jones* and the later series *Smith & Jones*. 1__ 2__

The Worst Week of My Life - 2004 to 2007 - Ben Miller stars with Sarah Alexander as the world's most disastrously awkward fiancé and husband. 1__ 2__ 3__ | Series 3 is a Christmas Special

The Worst Witch - 2017 to present - This young adult comedy follows an awkward girl witch who accidentally stumbles into witching school. 1__ 2__

The Wrong Mans - 2013 to 2014 - Two county council workers get mixed up in a case of mistaken identity, with chaotic results. 1__ 2__

The Young Offenders - 2018 to present - This coming-of-age comedy is about two teenage boys trying to steer clear of tough home lives and stay out of trouble. 1__

The Young Ones - 1982 to 1984 - Four strange and oddly-matched students attend college during the early 1980s. 1__ 2__

The Young Person's Guide to Becoming a Rock Star - 1998 - An emerging Scottish rock band has to face some hard realities on their way up the ladder. 1__

Thick as Thieves - 1974 - When burglar George is released from three years in prison, he finds his best friend has moved in with his wife, and he doesn't want to kick either of them out. 1__

This Country - 2017 to present - This sitcom looks at the lives of two young cousins living in The Cotswolds. 1__ 2__ 3__ | 2018 "The Aftermath"__

This is David Harper / This is David Lander - 1988 to 1990 - Stephen Fry and Tony Slattery each star in one season of this investigative journalism parody. 1__ 2__

This is Going to Hurt - 2019 to present - This comedy-drama series is based on Adam Kay's time as a junior doctor. 1___

Three Up, Two Down - 1985 to 1989 - Angie and Nick rent out their basement to her mother and his father, and it doesn't always go smoothly. 1___ 2___ 3___ 4___

Threesome - 2011 to 2012 - A straight couple and their gay friend live together happily until an unplanned encounter results in pregnancy. 1___ 2___

Time After Time - 1993 to 1995 - A convict attempts to go straight, but his family and friends aren't helping. 1___ 2___

Timewasters - 2017 to present - A struggling London jazz band is sent back in time to the 1920s. 1___ 2___

To the Manor Born - 1979 to 1981 - Penelope Keith stars in this series about an upper class woman forced to leave her home after her husband dies. 1___ 2___ 3___ | 2007 Christmas Special___

Together - 2015 - This short-lived sitcom focuses on a young couple in the early stages of their relationship. 1___

Tourist Trap - 2018 to present - This sitcom follows a team responsible for promoting Welsh tourism. 1___

Trevor's World of Sport - 2003 - This short-lived sitcom is set in the world of a sports PR firm. 1___

Tripper's Day - 1984 - A northern manager is assigned to run a very challenging London supermarket. 1___

Trivia - 2011 to 2012 - *Ireland* - A highly-dedicated quiz team leader in Ireland knows everything but how to deal with other people. 1___ 2___

Trollied - 2011 to 2018 - Manager Gavin takes pride in his work at Valco, but his employees don't always share the same enthusiasm. 1___ 2___ 3___ 4___ 5___ 6___ 7___ | Christmas Specials: 2012___ 2013___ 2015___ 2017___ 2018___

Two Doors Down - 2016 to present - A normal Glaswegian couple are extremely tolerant of their annoying neighbors who seem intent on showing up each day to disturb their quiet evenings. 1___ 2___ 3___ 4___ | 2017 Christmas Special___

Two in Clover - 1969 to 1970 - Two frustrated office workers leave their jobs for the simple life on a farm. 1___ 2___

Two Pints of Lager & a Packet of Crisps - 2001 to 2011 - In the northwestern town of Runcorn, a group of twentysomethings navigate early adulthood. 1___ 2___ 3___ 4___ 5___ 6___ 7___ 8___ 9___ | 2003 Musical Special___ 2009 Comic Relief___ 2009 "The Aftermath"___

Two's Company - 1975 to 1979 - A female American author has trouble getting along with her male British butler. 1___ 2___ 3___ 4___

Uncle - 2012 to 2017 - Andy is a man-child musician who has to grow up fast when he's called upon to take care of his nephew. 1___ 2___ 3___

Unfinished Business - 1998 to 1999 - After

two lovers leave her and shake her faith in relationships, a woman runs into the first man to hurt her so many years prior. 1___ 2___

Up Pompeii! - 1969 to 1970 - Lurcio is a slave in old Pompeii who spends most of his time trying to keep his owner's family from fighting. 1___ 2___

Upright - 2019 to present - *Australia* - Tim Minchin stars in this comedy about two misfits transporting an upright piano across Australia. 1___

Up the Elephant & Round the Castle - 1983 to 1985 - Jim inherits a rundown home, but runs into trouble from a neighbor, hateful councilors, and a squatter. 1___ 2___ 3___

Upstart Crow - 2016 to present - This sitcom gives us William Shakespeare, before he was famous. 1___ 2___ 3___ | 2017 Christmas Special___

Very British Problems - 2015 to 2016 - Comedians and celebrities what makes the British so different from other nationalities. 1___ 2___

Vicar of Dibley - 1994 to 2015 - When the 100-year-old Vicar of Dibley is replaced by a woman, some villagers are less than pleased. 1___ 2___ | The Easter Bunny___ The Christmas Lunch Incident___ Autumn___ Winter___ Spring___ Summer___ Merry Christmas___ Happy New Year___ The Handsome Stranger___ The Vicar in White___ | Comic Relief Specials: Ballykissdibley___ Celebrity Party___ Wife Swap___ Women Bishops___ The Bishop of Dibley___ Antiques Roadshow___

Vicious - 2013 to 2016 - An elderly gay couple takes great pleasure in socializing and insulting each other. 1___ 2___ | 2013 Christmas Special___ 2016 Special___

Village Hall - 1974 to 1975 - This anthology series focuses on what's happening in a village hall, and features early performances from actors like Zoë Wanamaker, Keith Clifford, Liz Smith, and Lesley Manville. 1___ 2___

W1A - 2014 to 2017 - This mockumentary-style show follows the new head of values at the BBC. 1___ 2___ 3___

Waiting for God - 1990 to 1994 - Two grumpy pensioners fall in love while biding their time in a retirement home. 1___ 2___ 3___ 4___ 5___ | Christmas Specials: 1992___ 1993___

Wannabe - 2018 to present - A former pop star becomes a highly incompetent music manager. 1___

Warren - 2019 to present - Martin Clunes stars as a grumpy driving instructor living in a situation he's none too happy with. 1___

Watching - 1987 to 1993 - This quirky comedy follows the romance between shy birdwatcher Malcolm and extrovert Brenda. 1___ 2___ 3___ 4___ 5___ 6___ 7___ | Christmas Specials: 1987___ 1988___ 1991___ | 1993 New Year's Special___

White Gold - 2017 to 2018* (on hold due to sexual misconduct allegations) - This unique comedy is about a group of window salesmen in early 1980s Essex. 1___

Whites - 2010 - Alan Davies stars as a chef

in a country hotel. 1___

Whoops Apocalypse - 1982 - This series takes a comedic look at the last week before the end of the world. 1___ | 1986 Movie___

Wild West - 2002 to 2004 - Two lesbians live in St. Gweep, exploring witchcraft and wife swapping. 1___ 2___

Witless - 2016 to present - Two young women are placed in witness protection after they see a murder. 1___ 2___ 3___

Year of the Rabbit - 2019 to present - This sitcom is set in Victorian London and focuses on boozehound DI Rabbit and his straight-laced partner. 1___

Yes Minister - 1980 to 1984 - James is a Cabinet Minister who thinks he's finally in a position to get things done. 1___ 2___ 3___ | 1982 Christmas Sketch___ 1984 Christmas Special___

Yes, Honestly - 1976 to 1977 - This sequel to *No, Honestly* saw Matthew Browne embarking on a relationship. 1___

Yes, Prime Minister - 1986 to 1988 - This follow-up to *Yes Minister* continues with the same cast but a new address on Downing Street. 1___ 2___

Yes, Prime Minister - 2013 - This revival of the much-loved *Yes Minister/Prime Minister* series featured a new cast and an economic downturn. 1___

Yonderland - 2013 to 2016 - Bored housewife Debbie opens her cupboard to a magical land where she is the Chosen One. 1___ 2___ 3___

You Rang, M'Lord - 1988 to 1993 - This period comedy is set in the 1920s and follows a wealthy widower and his band of servants. 1___ 2___ 3___ 4___

You, Me, & Them - 2013 to 2015 - Anthony Head and Eve Myles star in this sitcom about an age gap romance. 1___ 2___

You're Only Young Twice - 1977 to 1981 - Flora Petty and her sidekick Cissie terrorize the staff of the Paradise Lodge Retirement Home. 1___ 2___ 3___ 4___ | Christmas Specials: 1979___ 1980___

Young, Gifted, & Broke - 1999 to 2001 - A group of teens with pretty much no hope for a better life work together in an electrics company. 1___ 2___ 3___

Your Cheatin' Heart - 1990 - This comedy takes a look at the country music scene in Scotland. 1___

Yus, My Dear - 1976 - This *Romany Jones* sequel shows Wally and Lily after leaving their caravan for a new life in a council house. 1___

Zapped - 2016 to present - A West London temp worker is accidentally transported to the fantasy world of Munty, where he is trapped. 1___ 2___ 3___

100 Code - 2015 - Detective Tommy Conley travels to Stockholm to help a combative Swedish detective investigate a series of murders. 1___

55 Degrees North - 2004 to 2005 - After he alleges corruption against a colleague, a London detective moves to a new location. 1___ 2___

A Discovery of Witches - 2018 to present - A witch must solve a secret code with the help of an enigmatic vampire. 1___

A Dorothy L. Sayers Mystery - 1987 - This adaptation featured Edward Petherbridge as Lord Peter Wimsey, gentleman jewel thief. M___

A Fatal Inversion - 1992 - When bodies turn up at a country house Adam once owned, he's the obvious suspect. M___

A Game of Murder – 1966 - When a once-famous athlete dies mysteriously on a golf course, his detective son decides to investigate. 1___

A Mind to Kill - 1994 to 2002 - Philip Madoc stars as DCI Noel Bain, a Welsh detective who struggles a bit with the changing ways of police work. 1___ 2___ 3___ 4___ 5___ | 1998 Christmas Special___

A Most Mysterious Murder - 2005 - This miniseries was written by Julian Fellowes (*Downton Abbey*) and features real life unsolved murders told in docu-drama style. M___

A Mother's Son – 2012 - When a mother suspects her son of murder, she has to decide whether to turn him in or help cover it up. M___

A Place of Execution - 2009 - 45 years after a young girl disappears from a small English village, a journalist's documentary brings old events to the surface. M___

A Touch of Frost - 1992 to 2010 - Rumpled and slovenly DI Jack Frost follows his instincts to find justice for the underdogs. 1___ 2___ 3___ 4___ 5___ 6___ 7___ 8___ 9___ 10___ 11___ 12___ 13___ 14___ 15___

Above Suspicion - 2009 to 2012 - DC Anna Travis is a rookie detective determined to prove herself. 1___ 2___ 3___ 4___

Acceptable Risk - 2017 to present – When Sarah's husband is murdered, she realizes how little she knows about his past. 1___

Accused - 1996 - Each episode of this legal drama follows a single case in a busy magistrates' court. 1___

Accused - 2010 to 2012 - This series consists of self-contained episodes that look at how different people ended up in court. 1___ 2___

Ace of Wands - 1970 to 1972 - A stage magician named Tarot solves mysteries with his assistants. 1___ 2___

Afterlife - 2005 to 2006 - Before *The Walking Dead*, Andrew Lincoln starred in this British series about a university lecturer who's skeptical about the paranormal until meeting a medium. 1___ 2___

Agatha Christie Hour - 1982 - This series is a collection of one-hour dramas based on Agatha Christie's short stories. 1___

Agatha Christie's Poirot - 1989 to 2013 - The eccentric Belgian Detective Poirot investigates mysteries in this adaptation of the Agatha Christie classics. 1___ 2___ 3___ 4___ 5___ 6___ 7___ 8___ 9___ 10___ 11___ 12___ 13___

Agatha Raisin - 2014 to present - Based on the M.C. Beaton novels, Agatha Raisin leaves her high-flying London PR life for a peaceful existence in The Cotswolds - or so she thinks. 1___ 2___

Altered Carbon - 2018 to present - 360 years in the future, all consciousness is stored digitally and a rebel from the distant past is brought back and given a chance at a new life. 1___ 2___

Amber - 2014 - *Ireland* - Set in Dublin, this miniseries follows the disappearance of a 14-year-old girl named Amber. M___

Amnesia - 2004 - This miniseries tells the story of DS MacKenzie Stone, his tireless search for his wife who disappeared 5 years prior, and an amnesiac who factors into the case. M___

An Unsuitable Job for a Woman - 1997 to 2001 - Cordelia manages a rundown detective agency after her boss kills himself. 1___

And Then There Were None - 2015 - Based on the Agatha Christie novel, this miniseries sees 10 strangers invited to an island, only to be killed off one by one. M___

Appropriate Adult - 2011 - Based on the true story of Gloucester serial killer Fred West and his wife Rosemary West. M___

Armchair Mystery Theatre - 1960 to 1965 - This mystery anthology series was a spinoff from the drama anthology Armchair Theatre. 1___ 2___ 3___

Armchair Thriller - 1978 to 1982 - This anthology series features stories of mystery, suspense, and the supernatural. 1___ 2___

Arthur & George - 2015 - Martin Clunes stars as Sir Arthur Conan Doyle in this miniseries. M___

Ashes to Ashes - 2008 to 2010 - In this *Life on Mars* sequel, DCI Gene Hunt joins the Metro Police to work on "southern nancy" crimes with partner DI Alex Drake. 1___ 2___ 3___

Babylon - 2014 - This London-based series focuses on a number of high-ranking police officers and a new communications director in charge of improving police image. 1___

Backup - 1995 to 1997 - Nine men and women work in a special unit that does whatever is necessary to support the West Midlands Police Force. 1___ 2___

Bad Girls - 1999 to 2006 - This drama focuses on the inmates and staff in a fictional London-area prison. 1___ 2___ 3___ 4___ 5___ 6___ 7___ 8___

Badger - 1999 to 2000 - Tom and Jim are wildlife protection officers in Northumberland who investigate crimes related to wildlife. They work closely with Steph a vet, and Claire another officer. 1___ 2___

Bancroft - 2017 to 2018 - DS Elizabeth Bancroft is a brilliant officer, but the questionable tactics she employed in the past are coming back to haunt her. 1___ 2___

Bang - 2017 to present - In this bilingual Welsh crime drama, a man comes into possession of a gun and his life is forever changed. 1___

Baptiste - 2018 to present - Baptiste is a spinoff of the original series The Missing. 1___

Beasts - 1976 to 1976 - This supernatural anthology series was created in the 1970s and features six self-contained episodes of beastly horror – rats, witches, wolves, and...ghost dolphins terrorize the characters. 1___

Bedlam - 2011 to 2013 - A man with the ability to see ghosts moves to Bedlam Heights, home to numerous strange hauntings. 1___ 2___

Bergerac - 1981 to 1991 - Divorced alcoholic DS Jim Bergerac doesn't always do things the way his boss might prefer, but he gets results. 1___ 2___ 3___ 4___ 5___ 6___ 7___ 8___ 9___

Between the Lines - 1992 to 1994 - At the Complaints Investigation Bureau, they police the police. 1___ 2___ 3___

Births, Marriages, & Deaths - 1999 - A group of young men play a stag night prank on their old headmaster, and the consequences are disastrous. M___

Black Earth Rising - 2018 to present - Rescued as a child in Rwanda and now living in London, Kate Ashby takes on a case that will upend her life. 1___

Black Work - 2015 - A widowed policewoman tries to figure out who killed her husband during an undercover operation. 1___

Blackout - 2012 - A corrupt councilman awakens after an alcohol-induced blackout to realize he may have committed murder. M___

Blood Strangers - 2002 - This two-part crime drama stars Caroline Quentin (*Jonathan Creek*) as a mother whose daughter was killed while working as a teen prostitute. M___

Bloodlines - 2005 - A young policewoman's father has been in prison for murder. When he's released, she discovers a number of dark family secrets. M___

Blue Murder - 2003 to 2009 - DCI Janine Lewis struggles with the challenge of being a single mom to four kids while leading a team of detectives through homicide investigations. 1___ 2___ 3___ 4___ 5___

Bodyguard - 2018 to present - Police Sergeant David Budd is thrown into a conspiracy reaching the highest levels of British government. 1___

Boon - 1986 to 1995 - After suffering permanent lung damage rescuing a child from a fire, a fireman retires and begins a new life of odd jobs and later, detective work. 1___ 2___ 3___ 4___ 5___ 6___ 7___

Born to Kill - 2017 - In this miniseries, a teenager harbors dark and psychopathic desires. M___

Broadchurch - 2013 to 2017 - When an 11-year-old boy is murdered in a quiet coastal community, town secrets are exposed. 1___ 2___ 3___

Bulman - 1985 to 1987 - An ex-cop retires to repair clocks in an antique and junk shop, but it doesn't take much for the daughter of an old colleague to convince him to become partners in a PI firm. 1___ 2___

In addition to starring in Broadchurch, David Tennant also starred in its American adaptation, Gracepoint. Chris Chibnall created both.

Burnside - 2000 - This spinoff of *The Bill* follows DCI Frank Burnside as he goes to work for the National Crime Squad. 1___

By Any Means - 2013 - This series follows a clandestine investigative unit that operates in gray areas to get the job done. 1___

Cadfael - 1994 to 1998 - A monk named Cadfael solves medieval mysteries in Shrewsbury. 1___ 2___ 3___ 4___

Callan - 1965 to 1972 - David Callan is a reluctant assassin for a shadowy branch of British Intelligence. 1___ 2___ 3___ 4___

Campion - 1989 to 1990 - An aristocrat in the 1930s adopts a fake name and investigates mysteries with help from his servant. 1___ 2___

Cardinal - 2017 to present - Police detectives John Cardinal and Lise Delorme investigate crimes in Algonquin Bay. 1___ 2___

Case Histories - 2011 to 2013 - Based on the Jackson Brodie novels by Kate Atkinson, this Edinburgh-based series features a tough guy PI with a heart of gold. 1___ 2___

Case Sensitive - 2011 to 2012 - DS Zailer and DC Waterhouse take different perspectives on the murder of a mother and her 5-year-old daughter. 1___ 2___

Catweazle - 1970 to 1971 - An 11th-century wizard falls through time and lands in 1969, where he befriends a young boy. 1___ 2___

Chancer - 1990 to 1991 - Clive Owen stars as "Dex", a successful businessman with a shady past. 1___ 2___

Chandler & Co - 1994 to 1995 - A housewife and a divorcee become private detectives, solving cases and finding themselves. 1___ 2___

Charters & Caldicott - 1985 - Two retired gentleman set out to solve a murder and end up involved in espionage. M___

Chasing Shadows - 2014 - A difficult but gifted officer works within a missing persons unit to find cases that may be linked to murder. 1___

Children of the North – 1991 - When two MI6 officers are killed in an unmarked car, all manner of chaos rains down. 1___

Chimera - 1991 - When his girlfriend dies at a fertility clinic, a journalist investigates. 1___

Circles of Deceit - 1993 to 1996 - This series of 4 made-for-TV films features Dennis Waterman as John Neil, a war hero turned special operative acting as a lone agent on tough cases. 1___

City Central - 1998 to 2000 - This series looks at the public and private lives of the men and women who work the City Central police station in Manchester. 1___ 2___ 3___

Class - 2016 - *This Doctor Who* spinoff is set in the fictional Coal Hill Academy, where students deal with all the normal issues, plus the pressures of time travel. 1___

Clean Break - 2015 - *Ireland* - Car dealer Frank Mallon's life is in shambles, but he devises a plan to solve his money problems and get revenge on the people making his life miserable. 1___

Close & True - 2000 - An inexperienced lawyer works in a rundown office. 1___

Code of a Killer - 2015 - This criminal drama tells the story of the first time DNA fingerprinting was used to help solve a murder case. 1___

Cold Blood - 2005 to 2008 - A notorious murderer is finally placed in prison, but they can't find his last victim. 1___ 2___

Collateral - 2018 to present - When a pizza delivery man is murdered, police soon realize there's much more to the story. 1___

Collision - 2009 - A major road accident changes the lives of several people who had never met prior to the incident. 1___

Colonel March of Scotland Yard - 1954 to 1956 - This vintage series stars Boris Karloff as a detective who investigates unusual and sometimes supernatural cases. 1___

Conviction - 2004 - Mistakes made during the investigation of a 12-year-old girl's murder have consequences for the investigators. 1___

Cracker - 1993 to 1996 - Though he's obnoxious and anti-social, Fitz is a brilliant criminal psychologist and police consultant. 1___ 2___ 3___

Crime Stories - 2012 - This heavily improvised crime drama features a former real-life police officer investigating crimes

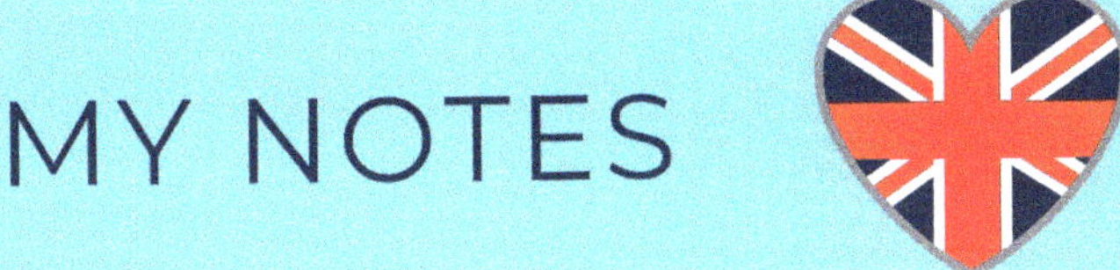
MY NOTES

alongside well-known guest actors. 1__

Crime Traveler - 1997 - A detective and scientist team up to travel back in time to solve crimes. 1__

Criminal Justice - 2008 to 2009 - Each series follows a different case through the justice system. 1__ 2__

Crown Court - 1972 to 1984 - There are nearly 900 episodes of this legal drama about the court proceedings in fictional Fulchester. 1__ 2__ 3__ 4__ 5__ 6__ 7__ 8__ 9__ 10__ 11__

Crownies - 2011 - This series was a predecessor to *Janet King*, and it focused on lawyers working for the crown prosecution service. 1__

Cuffs - 2015 - *Cuffs* takes a look at the lives of front-line police officers in seaside Brighton and surrounding areas in Sussex. 1__

Dalziel & Pascoe - 1996 to 2007 - Police partners with very different personalities find a way to bond as they solve crimes. 1__ 2__ 3__ 4__ 5__ 6__ 7__ 8__ 9__ 10__ 11__ 12__

Danger Man - 1960 to 1968 - John Drake is a secret agent whose assignments frequently require him to oversee the preservation of world peace. 1__ 2__ 3__

Dark Angel - 2016 - This miniseries tells the story of Mary Ann Cotton, an English serial killer who may or may not have killed several of her husbands and most of her children. M__

Dark Heart - 2018 to present - DI Wagstaffe leads an investigation into a series of attacks on accused pedophiles. 1__

Dark Realm - 2000 to 2001 - This horror anthology was filmed entirely on the Isle of Man. 1__

Daylight Robbery - 1999 to 2000 - When four housewives find themselves in financial difficulties, they plan a robbery. 1__ 2__

DCI Banks - 2010 to 2016 - Stephen Tompkinson stars as DCI Alan Banks, a stubborn but competent investigator in Yorkshire. 1__ 2__ 3__ 4__ 5__

Death Comes to Pemberley - 2013 to 2014 - A couple is enjoying their 6th anniversary party when something happens to stop it dead. 1__

Death in Paradise - 2011 to present - A British inspector who's fundamentally incompatible with island life is sent to investigate murders on a tropical island. 1__ 2__ 3__ 4__ 5__ 6__ 7__ 8__

Deceit - 2000 - Based on the novel by Clare Francis, *Deceit* tells the story of a housewife whose husband mysteriously goes missing after a sailing excursion on his yacht. M__

Deep Water - 2016 - When a young gay man is murdered, investigators find a link to a string of gay murders in the 1980s and 90s. M__

Demons - 2009 - Luke is just a normal teenage boy until a family friend reveals he's actually the great-grandson of famed vampire hunter Abraham Van Helsing. 1__

Dempsey and Makepeace - 1985 to 1986 - When a tough NYPD cop is partnered with a sexy Londoner, sparks fly. 1___ 2___ 3___

Department S - 1969 to 1970 - A trio of quirky agents takes on cases others have failed to solve. 1___ 2___

Dirk Gently - 2010 to 2012 – An unusual detective looks to the universe for holistic solutions to mysteries. 1___

DNA - 2004 to 2006 - After a nervous breakdown, criminologist Joe Donovan returns to lead the Forensic Investigations Unit in Manchester. 1___

Doctor Blake Mysteries - 2013 to present - *Australia* - After 30 years away, the eccentric Doctor Lucien Blake returns home to Ballarat to take over his late father's medical practice and role as police surgeon. 1___ 2___ 3___ 4___ 5___

Doing Money - 2019 to present - This series tells the story of Ana, a young Romanian woman kidnapped in London and sold into sex slavery. M___

Dracula - 2013 to 2014 - This British-American series shows Dracula coming to London as an American entrepreneur with ulterior motives. 1___

East West 101 - 2007 to 2011 - *Australia* - Malik and Crowley are a study in opposites as they investigate major crimes. 1___ 2___ 3___

Edge of Darkness - 1985 - A police inspector investigates the murder of his daughter, an environmental activist. M___

Endeavor - 2013 to present - In this prequel to *Inspector Morse*, a young Endeavour works with Sergeant Thursday to develop his investigative skills. 1___ 2___ 3___ 4___ 5___ 6 _ | 2012 Movie___

Escape into Night - 1972 - Confined to bed, a young girl draws an imaginary world she's then able to explore in her dreams - until one night when she finds someone else in her world. 1___

Eternal Law - 2012 - Two angels are sent to York to assist in court cases. 1___

Exile - 2011 - John Simm (*Life on Mars*) stars in this drama about a man who returns to his hometown after his career implodes, only to find an unfolding mystery that's complicated by his father's Alzheimer's. 1___

Falcón - 2012 - This short series was set in Seville, Spain and based on the crime novels of Robert Wilson. 1___

Father Brown - 2013 to present - Based

on the mysteries of GK Chesterson, a Catholic priest solves mysteries in his small English village. 1__ 2__ 3__ 4__ 5__ 6__ | Christmas Specials: 2016__ 2017__

Father Brown - 1974 - A Catholic priest dips his toe into mysteries in spite of the police warning him off. 1__

Fearless - 2017 to 2018 - When human rights lawyer Emma Banville attempts to overturn a convicted murderer's case, she finds a deeper conspiracy than she bargained for. 1__

Finney - 1994 - When the patriarch of a crime family is killed, the search is on to find out who did it. 1__

Five Daughters - 2010 - Set in 2006, this series is about the five victims of the Ipswich serial murders. M__

Five Days - 2007 to 2010 - A young mother disappears and abandons her children. 1__ 2__

Floodtide - 1987 to 1988 - Set in England and France, this series dives into the world of international cocaine smuggling. 1__ 2__

Forgotten - 1999 - A man is living a peaceful life in the English countryside until a reminder from his past unsettles things. M__

Fortitude - 2015 to present - On an Arctic Norwegian island, a strange parasite has survived in the ice for thousands of years. 1__ 2__

Fox - 1980 - This early 80s series revolves around the gang-connected South London Fox family. 1__

Foyle's War - 2002 to 2015 - DCS Foyle fights a war against crime in southern England as WWII goes on around him. 1__ 2__ 3__ 4__ 5__ 6__ 7__ 8__

Fraud Squad - 1969 to 1970 - Two investigators seek out conmen and fraudsters at all levels of society. 1__ 2__

From Darkness - 2015 - In Greater Manchester, Officer Claire is disturbed by four bodies that seem linked to her past cases. 1__

Frontiers - 1996 - This short-lived crime drama focuses on a rivalry between two police chiefs and their teams. 1__

Gangs of London - 2019 to present - This big-budget series will be set in a version of London that's been torn apart by all manner of international criminal organizations. 1__

Ghost Squad - 1961 to 1964 - The Ghost Squad is a division of Scotland Yard dealing in situations too sensitive or challenging for ordinary investigators. 1__ 2__ 3__

Gideon's Way - 1964 to 1967 - This series examines the public and private life of Commander George Gideon of Scotland Yard. 1__ 2__

Glue - 2014 - When a teenage boy is killed, the subsequent investigation draws out all manner of village secrets. 1__

Good Cop - 2012 - When his best friend is killed, a good cop wants revenge. 1__

Good Omens - 2019 - Based on the Terry Pratchett and Neil Gaiman novel, this series tells the tale of a severely bungled apocalypse. M___

Grantchester - 2015 to present - A village clergyman helps a local police detective solve crimes. 1___ 2___ 3___ 4___ | 2016 Christmas Special___

Hamish MacBeth - 1995 to 1997 - Hamish Macbeth is a talented but unambitious Highlands constable who doesn't always follow the rules. 1___ 2___ 3___

Happy Valley - 2014 to 2019 - Sarah Lancashire stars as a troubled police sergeant investigating crimes in West Yorkshire. 1___ 2___ 3___

Hard Sun - 2018 - While investigating a murder in contemporary London, two detectives stumble upon evidence that the world will be destroyed in 5 years - evidence the government is trying to hide. 1___

Harry - 2013 - Detective Harry Anglesea returns to work just four weeks after his wife's suicide, and it may be too soon. 1___

Hazell - 1978 to 1979 - *New Zealand* - Edgy but charismatic private detective James Hazell investigates mysteries. 1___ 2___

He Kills Coppers - 2008 - Based on a novel by Jake Arnott, this three-part drama explores the death of three police officers during the 1966 World Cup celebrations. M___

Hetty Wainthropp Investigates - 1996 to 1998 - A tough old pensioner becomes a private detective and investigates crimes with the help of her husband and a teenage boy called Geoffrey. 1___ 2___ 3___ 4___ | Missing Persons Movie___

Hidden - 2011 - When a man agrees to help find a missing alibi witness, he's unintentionally drawn into a much larger conspiracy. M___

Hidden aka Craith - 2018 to present - This bilingual Welsh drama focuses on an investigation following the discovery of a missing young woman's body in a nearby lake. 1___

Him - 2016 - A boy known only as HIM discovers he has telekinetic powers. M___

Hinterland - 2013 to 2016 - In Wales, DCI Tom Mathias investigates crimes while trying to move beyond problems in his past. 1___ 2___ 3___

Hit & Miss - 2012 - This Paul Abbott-created series stars Chloë Sevigny as a transgender contract killer. 1___

Holding On - 1997 - The murder of a young woman in London acts as a catalyst to draw a group of unconnected people together. 1___

Honest - 2008 - Amanda Redman stars as a woman whose husband has spent several years in prison, and all she wants to do is get her family on the straight and narrow. 1___

Houdini & Doyle - 2016 - The police look outside their regular sources to people like Harry Houdini and Arthur Conan Doyle to help them solve crimes. 1___

Humans - 2015 to present - Based on the Swedish show *Real Humans*, this series explores ideas around AI and robotics. 1___ 2___

Hunted - 2012 - After an attempt on her life, a spy goes back undercover as a nanny, unsure of who she can trust. 1___

Identity - 2010 - Aidan Gillen and Keeley Hawes star in this police procedural about a unit specializing in identity fraud. 1___

In Plain Sight - 2016 - This series covers serial killer Peter Manue's crimes in 1950s Lanarkshire, Scotland. M___

In the Club - 2014 to 2016 - This drama follows six couples who attended parenting classes during their pregnancies. 1___ 2___

In the Dark - 2017 - While dealing with an unexpected pregnancy, DI Weeks returns to her hometown to help a childhood friend after an abduction. M___

In the Flesh - 2013 to 2014 - The government attempts to rehabilitate the undead for a return to normal society. 1___ 2___

Informer - 2018 to present - A London counter-terrorism officer convinces a young Pakistani man to go undercover as an informant for him. 1___

Injustice - 2011 - A defense barrister has to deal with the consequences of defending an indefensible crime. 1___

Innocent - 2018 to present - When David Collins's conviction for murdering his wife is overturned, he struggles to recover his broken world. 1___

Inside Men - 2012 - This four-part miniseries follows an armed robbery at a secure counting house in Bristol. 1___

Inspector Alleyn Mysteries - 1990 to 1994 - Set in the late 1930s, this series follows DCI Roderick Alleyn as he investigates murders. 1___ 2___

Inspector George Gently - 2007 to 2017 - Inspector George Gently and DS Bacchus chase criminals in the 1960's in Northeast England. 1___ 2___ 3___ 4___ 5___ 6___ 7___ 8___

Inspector Morse - 1987 to 2000 - Grumpy, classical music-loving Inspector Morse investigates crimes around Oxford with his junior partner Sergeant Lewis. 1___ 2___ 3___ 4___ 5___ 6___ 7___ 8___ 9___ 10___ 11___ 12___

Interpol Calling - 1959 to 1960 - Interpol inspector Paul Duval chases criminals around the globe. 1___

Ironside - 2013 - A tough police detective tied to a wheelchair pushes his staff to bring in the clues that will solve their cases. 1___

Jack Irish - 2012 to 2018 - *Australia* - Jack Irish is a talented PI with a checkered past. 1___ 2___ | TV Movies: Bad Debts___ Black Tide___ Dead Point___

Jack Taylor - 2010 to 2016 - Resistant to rules, ex-cop Jack Taylor becomes a private investigator after losing his job with the Guard. 1___ 2___ 3___

Janet King - 2014 to 2017 - *Australia* - This spinoff from the legal drama *Crownies* follows Senior Crown Prosecutor Janet King as she returns from maternity leave and progresses through her career. 1___ 2___ 3___

Jekyll - 2007 - James Nesbitt (*Cold Feet*)

stars in this modern-day variation on the Jekyll and Hyde story. 1___

Jekyll & Hyde - 2015 - The grandson of Dr. Henry Jekyll has inherited his grandfather's alter ego and personality problems. 1___

Jemima Shore Investigates - 1983 - Patricia Hodge (*Miranda*) stars in this series about a TV presenter who also dabbles in amateur sleuthing. 1___

Jericho of Scotland Yard - 2005 - This period mystery gives us DI Michael Jericho, a WWII veteran who investigates murders while also seeking to figure out the circumstances surrounding his father's death. M___

Jo - 2013 - Commander Jo Saint-Clair leads a team of detectives in Paris, though the entire series is in English. 1___

Jonathan Creek - 1997 to 2016 - After meeting a pushy investigative journalist, an eccentric magic trick developer also finds himself solving murders. 1___ 2___ 3___ 4___ 5___ | Christmas Specials: 1998___ 2001___ | The Grinning Man (2009)___ The Judas Tree (2010)___ 2013 The Clue of the Savant's Thumb (2013)___

Jonathan Strange & Mr. Norrell - 2015 - Enigmatic recluse Mr. Norrell and fledgling magician Jonathan Strange bring magic back to Britain. 1___

Judge John Deed - 2001 to 2007 - Judge John Deed is no ordinary judge, and he often finds himself in trouble because of it. 1___ 2___ 3___ 4___ 5___ 6___

Kat & Alfie: Redwater - 2017 - 32 years after giving her son up for adoption, Kat moves to the town of Redwater in an attempt to find him. 1___

Kavanagh QC - 1995 to 2001 - John Thaw (*Inspector Morse*) stars as an old barrister with a demanding job and an equally demanding home life. 1___ 2___ 3___ 4___ 5___ 6___

Keeping Faith - 2017 to present - A Welsh lawyer cuts her maternity leave short when her husband goes missing. 1___ 2___

Kidnap & Ransom - 2011 to 2012 - This series follows the work of a British hostage negotiator. 1___ 2___

Killer Net - 1998 - A psychology student becomes obsessed with a computer game about murder, but it gets scary when it suddenly seems to be connected to real murders. M___

Killing Eve - 2018 to present - An underutilized MI5 officer pursues an elusive female assassin. 1___ 2___

Kiri - 2018 to present - Sarah Lancashire (*Happy Valley*) stars as a social worker on the case of Kiri, a young black girl who's abducted just before her adoption by a white family. 1___

Kiss Me First - 2018 to present - Two girls become friends in the virtual world of an online game, and one is pulled into something much darker than she had imagined. 1___

Law and Order: UK - 2009 to 2014 - This series is an adaptation of the popular

American police and court procedural drama. 1___ 2___ 3___ 4___ 5___ 6___ 7___ 8___

Lewis aka Inspector Lewis - 2006 to 2015 - This sequel to *Inspector Morse* picks up where its predecessor left off, with Inspector Lewis heading up challenging investigations around Oxford. 1___ 2___ 3___ 4___ 5___ 6___ 7___ 8___ 9___

Liar - 2017 to present - After a woman's rapist gets away due to lack of evidence, she takes matters into her own hands. 1___ 2___

Life of Crime - 2013 - A rookie cop chases a young girl's killer for nearly 30 years. M___

Life on Mars - 2006 to 2007 - DCI Sam Tyler has a car accident in 2006 and wakes up in the 70s. 1___ 2___

Lightfields - 2013 - *Lightfields* is a miniseries follow-up to *Marchlands*, in which a tragic death in 1944 leaves a presence that affects all those who eventually live in the haunted home. M___

Like Father Like Son - 2005 - Things seem to be looking up for one single mother with a dark past, but then her son learns the truth about his father. M___

> Before Neil Dudgeon was DCI John Barnaby, he was Daniel Bolt, the lusty Midsomer gardener from Series 4, Episode 1: Garden of Death.

Line of Duty - 2012 to present - DS Arnot from the Anti-Corruption Unit investigates a popular DCI after a mistaken shooting. 1___ 2___ 3___ 4___ 5___ 6___

Little Boy Blue - 2017 - This miniseries tells the story of a young Liverpudlian boy's murder and how his killer was brought to justice. M___

London Spy - 2015 to 2015 - A brief romance between two very different men draws one of them into a dark world after the other is murdered. M___

Lord Peter Wimsey - 1972 to 1975 - This series is made up of five feature-length television movies starring Ian Carmichael as Lord Peter Wimsey. M___

Lovejoy - 1986 to 1994 - Ian McShane stars as Lovejoy, the slightly shady antiques dealer and part-time detective. 1___ 2___ 3___ 4___ 5___ 6___

Luther - 2010 to present - Idris Elba stars in this gritty series about a brilliant London-based detective whose personal feelings and passions often get him in trouble. 1___ 2___ 3___ 4___ 5___

M.R. James Ghost Stories - 2005 to 2010 - This collection is made up of three ghost story adaptations: *Whistle and I'll Come to You*, *A View from a Hill*, and *Number 13*. M___

Mad Dogs - 2011 to 2013 - John Simm and Philip Glenister (both of *Life on*

Mars) reunite alongside Max Beesley and Marc Warren in this psychological thriller about old friends gathering in Spain and getting caught up in a world of corruption. 1__ 2__ 3__ 4__

Maelstrom - 1985 - Shortly after being made redundant, an English woman learns she's been left a fortune in Norway, but her efforts to figure out lead to bad things. M__

Maigret - 1992 to 1993 - Maigret keeps his sense of humor as he examines the dark motives behind the crimes. 1__ 2__

Maigret - 2016 to 2018 - Rowan Atkinson stars in this adaptation of the popular French detective. 1__ 2__

Malice Aforethought - 1979 - A doctor believes he has committed the perfect murder of his wife. 1__

Man in a Suitcase - 1967 to 1968 - A US agent is thrown out of the agency for something he didn't do, so he travels around Europe working as a PI and trying to clear his name. 1__

Manhunt - 2018 to present - This crime drama is based on the real-life capture of serial killer Levi Bellfield. 1__

Marcella - 2016 to present - After Marcella leaves her job as a detective to concentrate on family, her husband leaves her for another woman and she decides to return to the force. 1__ 2__ 3__

Marchlands - 2011 - Jodie Whittaker (*Doctor Who, Broadchurch*) stars in this miniseries set at three different points in time at one haunted house. M__

Masterpiece Mystery - 1980 to 2016 - This weekly anthology program offers British mysteries for the American public, featuring Vincent Price, Diana Rigg, Gene Shalit, and Alan Cumming as hosts. 1__ 2__ 3__ 4__ 5__ 6__ 7__ 8__ 9__ 10__ 11__ 12__ 13__ 14__ 15__ 16__ 17__ 18__ 19__ 20__ 21__ 22__ 23__ 24__ 25__ 26__ 27__ 28__ 29__ 30__ 31__ 32__ 33__ 34__ 35__ 36__ 37__ 38__ 39__ 40__ 41__ 42__ 43__ 44__

Mayday - 2013 - When the May Queen disappears just before May Day celebrations, a small town is thrown into chaos. 1__

McCallum - 1995 to 1998 - Pathologist McCallum and his team help the dead tell their stories. 1__ 2__

McCready & Daughter - 2001 - *Ireland* - When his daughter drops out of university, she joins her father as a private investigator in an Irish community. 1__ | 2000 Movie__

Messiah - 2001 to 2008 - This miniseries collection features Ken Stott leading a team of serial killer investigators, but later switches to Marc Warren. 1__ 2__ 3__ 4__ 5__

MI-5 aka Spooks - 2002 to 2011 - This dramatic series follows top secret missions of the MI-5, the UK's elite domestic security and counter-intelligence agency. 1__ 2__ 3__ 4__ 5__ 6__ 7__ 8__ 9__ 10__

Midsomer Murders - 1997 to 2018 - DCI Barnaby solves murders in the not-so-peaceful British countryside. 1__ 2__ 3__ 4__ 5__ 6__ 7__ 8__ 9__ 10__ 11__ 12__ 13__ 14__ 15__ 16__ 17__ 18__ 19__ 20__

| 2008 Documentary__ | Christmas Specials: 2004__ 2008__ 2013__

Midwinter of the Spirit - 2015 - Country Vicar Merrily Watkins consults on a murder investigation and gets on-the-job training in exorcism. M__

Miss Fisher's Murder Mysteries - 2012 to 2015 - In the 1920s, Miss Phryne Fisher works as a skilled private detective. 1__ 2__ 3__

Miss Marple - 2004 to 2014 - In the small village of St. Mary Mead, Miss Marple helps her community by solving murders. 1__ 2__ 3__ 4__ 5__ 6__

Missing - 2009 to 2010 - In a busy missing persons unit, DS Mary Croft leads a determined but under-resourced team. 1__ 2__

Mitch - 1984 to 1984 - John Thaw (*Inspector Morse*) stars as a reporter who covers the most unsavory of crimes. 1__ 2__ 3__ 4__

Moses Jones - 2009 - A body found in the Thames seems to be related to witchcraft. M__

Mother Love - 1989 to 1989 - An otherwise pleasant marriage turns ugly when a jealous mother-in-law gets in the middle of things. M__

Mr. and Mrs. Murder - 2013 - *Australia* - A married couple runs an industrial cleaning business while also solving murders. 1__

Mr. Palfrey of Westminster - 1984 to 1985 - Mr. Palfrey seems to be a typical, mild-mannered government employee, but he's actually a spook. 1__ 2__

Mrs. Bradley Mysteries - 1998 to 2000 - Diana Rigg stars as Mrs. Bradley, a sort of edgy Miss Marple who solves mysteries with the assistance of her devoted chauffeur. 1__

Murder - 2012 to 2016 - This unusually-filmed series shows the events up to and after a number of different murders, with each episode offering a self-contained story. 1__

Murder City - 2005 to 2006 - Kris Marshall (*Death in Paradise*) stars in this series about two mismatched London detectives who solve complicated cases. 1__ 2__

Murder in Mind - 2001 to 2003 - Each episode in this anthology series features a murder from the killer's perspective. 1__ 2__ 3__

Murder in Suburbia - 2004 to 2005 - Posh Ash and working-class Scribbs solve murders in the fictional suburban town of Middleford. 1__ 2__

Murder in Successville - 2015 to 2017 - Each episode features a celebrity teamed with DI Sleet to investigate a crime in a town filled that's also filled with celebrities. 1__ 2__ 3__

Murder Investigation Team - 2003 to 2005 - A London-based team of elite investigators handles exceptionally challenging murders. 1__ 2__

Murder Most English: The Flaxborough Chronicles - 1977 - This

MY NOTES

1970s detective series is based on the Flaxborough novels by Colin Watson.1___

Murder Most Horrid - 1991 to 1999 - In each episode, the lead actress plays a different character investigating a different murder, written by a different writer. 1___ 2___ 3___ 4___

Murder on the Homefront - 2013 - This two-part miniseries follows a doctor and his receptionist as they investigate a serial killer in the midst of the blitz. M___

Murderland - 2009 - This miniseries looks at a murder from the perspectives of the daughter, the detective, and the murder victim. M___

Murdoch Mysteries - 2008 to present - *Canada* - Set in the 1890s, Murdoch uses early forensics to solve murders. 1___ 2___ 3___ 4___ 5___ 6___ 7___ 8___ 9___ 10___ 11___ 12___ 13___ | TV Movies: Except the Dying___ Poor Tom is Cold___ Under the Dragon's Tail___ | Christmas Specials: 2004___ 2013___ 2017___

Murphy's Law - 2001 to 2007 - James Nesbitt (*Cold Feet*) stars as Tommy Murphy, a charming but tough Northern Irish cop with a tragic past. 1___ 2___ 3___ 4___ 5___

The building used as the restaurant in Pie in the Sky housed a dollhouse maker after the series ended. Frankly, that sounds like another great setting for a murder mystery.

My Cousin Rachel - 1983 - Based on the Daphne du Maurier novel, a man becomes convinced his wife has murdered his friend. M___

Mystery Road - 2018 to present - *Australia* - Detective Jay Swan investigates crimes in the Australian Outback. 1___ 2___ | 2013 Movie___

New Blood - 2016 to present - Two young investigators are brought together by cases that initially appear unrelated. 1___

New Scotland Yard - 1972 to 1974 - Two detectives solve the big cases for the New Scotland Yard. 1___ 2___ 3___ 4___

New Tricks - 2003 to 2015 - Retired police officers are called back to investigate old cold cases. 1___ 2___ 3___ 4___ 5___ 6___ 7___ 8___ 9___ 10___ 11___ 12___

No Offence - 2015 to present - This gritty Manchester-based police drama showcases the work of investigators under straight-talking DI Viv Deering. 1___ 2___ 3___

Nobody's House - 1976 - Two children move into an old Victorian house with their parents, and only they can see its ghostly inhabitant. 1___

One of Us - 2016 - In a remote Scottish Village, childhood sweethearts are found murdered after returning home from their honeymoon. M___

Ordeal by Innocence - 2018 - This three-part drama is based on the Agatha

Christie novel of the same name. M___

Our Friends in the North - 1996 - This miniseries follows four friends from the heady 60s to the not-so-certain 90s. M___

Out - 1978 - After doing time for a bank robbery gone wrong, Frank will stop at nothing to find out who got him sent to jail. 1___

Out of the Blue - 1995 to 1996 - Neil Dudgeon and John Hannah star in this gritty drama about a group of police at Brazen Gate CID. 1___ 2___

P.D. James: Death in Holy Orders - 2003 - Detective Adam Dalgliesh looks into an old murder case at Saint Anselm's, and another murder occurs while he's there. M___

P.D. James: The Murder Room - 2004 - When a man is killed in a manner that mirrors an exhibit in his family's museum, Detective Adam Dalgliesh investigates. M___

Paranoid - 2016 - A playground murder with witnesses takes detectives into a dark mystery that sends them across Europe in search of the killer. M___

Partners in Crime - 2015 - Jessica Raine and David Walliams star as Tommy and Tuppence, solving mysteries in 1950s Britain. M___

Partners in Crime - 1983 to 1984 - Francesca Annis and James Warwick star in this take on Agatha Christie's Tommy & Tuppence mysteries. 1___ 2___

Paula - 2017 to present - A chance hookup turns a woman's life upside down. 1___

Penny Dreadful - 2014 to 2016 - A group of explorers and adventurers team up to fight supernatural threats in Victorian England. 1___ 2___ 3___

Picnic at Hanging Rock - 2018 - *Australia* - On Valentine's Day 1900, three schoolgirls and their governess go missing. M___

Pie in the Sky - 1994 to 1997 - When DI Crabbe leaves the police force to open a restaurant, they continue to pull him back in for part-time crime-solving. 1___ 2___ 3___ 4___ 5___

Pine Gap - 2018 to present - *Australia* - This spy thriller takes place at a joint US/ Australian defence facility in Australia. 1___

Place of Execution - 2009 - 45 years after a young girl disappears from an English village, a journalist attempts to make a documentary on the subject and causes more trouble than intended. M___

Prey - 2014 to 2015 - Manchester Detective Marcus Farrow (John Simm of Life on Mars) is accused of a crime he didn't commit, sending him on the run as he tries to prove his innocence. 1___ 2___

Prime Suspect - 1991 to 2006 - Helen Mirren stars as Detective Jane Tennison, battling crime as well as sexism on the job. 1___ 2___ 3___ 4___ 5___ 6___ 7___

Prime Suspect 1973 - 2017 - This *Prime Suspect* prequel explores the beginning of Jane Tennison's career as a police officer, along with her first murder case. 1___

Primeval - 2007 to 2011 - Prehistoric creatures begin to appear in England, so Professor Cutter and his team are dispatched to capture them. 1___ 2___ 3___ 4___ 5___

Prisoners' Wives - 2012 - Gemma thinks she has a perfect life until her husband is arrested for murder. 1___ 2___

Proof - 2004 to 2005 - When an investigative reporter discovers a connection between two crimes, he unearths much more than expected. 1___ 2___

Public Enemies - 2012 - Anna Friel (*Marcella*) stars in this series about a probation officer helping a convicted murderer adjust to life back on the outside. M___

Quatermass - 1979 - This science fiction series shows us a broken-down civilization where an alien power appears to be influencing the young. 1___

Quirke - 2013 to 2014 - Gabe Byrne plays a pathologist in 1950s Dublin. 1___

Raffles - 1975 to 1977 - In Edwardian England, A.J. Raffles is a gentleman of leisure, but he's also an accomplished safecracker and jewel thief. 1___

Randall & Hopkirk (Deceased) - 1969 to 1970 - Two private detectives, one living and one dead, work together to figure out who killed Hopkirk. 1___

Randall & Hopkirk (Deceased) - 2000 to 2001 - Two detectives solve mysteries, but one of them is a ghost. 1___ 2___

Rebus - 2000 to 2004 - Based on the novels of Scottish author Ian Rankin, Inspector Rebus is an old-fashioned detective in every sense of the word. He smokes, drinks, and doesn't have a lot of luck with his personal life. 1___ 2___ 3___ 4___

Reilly: Ace of Spies - 1983 - Sam Neill plays Sidney Reilly, the legendary British spy who inspired James Bond. M___

Rellik - 2017 to present - DCI Markham and his team hunt down a killer in this mystery told in reverse. M___

Remember Me - 2014 - A man moves into a retirement facility and promptly becomes sole witness to a murder. M___

Republic of Doyle - 2010 to 2014 - *Canada* - Jake and Malachy Doyle run a questionable private investigations firm in Newfoundland. 1___ 2___ 3___ 4___ 5___ 6___

Requiem - 2018 to present - More than 20 years after a child disappears in Wales, a seemingly unrelated suicide draws a young woman back to the village where it happened. 1___

Residue - 2015 to present - Journalist Jennifer Preston seeks the truth in a futuristic English city, often finding paranormal answers. 1___

Rillington Place - 2016 - This miniseries tells the story of serial killer John Christie, a man who killed at least seven women in the 40s and 50s. M___

Ripper Street - 2012 to 2017 - DI Reid and his team police the streets of Whitechapel where Jack the Ripper once roamed. 1___ 2___ 3___ 4___ 5___

Rebus author Ian Rankin has never seen the television adaptations of his work. He's expressed concern that it might change the way he writes the character.

River - 2015 - River is a brilliant but haunted detective. 1___

Riviera - 2017 to present - An American woman finds herself mixed up in a world of lies and crime when she attempts to find out the truth about her husband's death. 1___ 2___

Rockliffe's Babies aka Rockliffe's Folly - 1987 to 1988 - A tough, old-school detective is charged with seven CID trainees. 1___ 2___

Rose & Maloney - 2002 to 2005 - Sarah Lancashire (*Happy Valley*) stars as a woman who works at the Criminal Justice Review Agency, fighting miscarriages of justice. 1___ 2___ 3___

Rosemary & Thyme - 2003 to 2008 - Former policewoman Laura and a horticulture professor Rosemary are brought together by a love of gardening, but murder seems to follow them. 1___ 2___ 3___

Rough Diamond aka Diamond Geezer - 2005 to 2007 - David Jason (*A Touch of Frost*) stars as a professional jewel thief using his abilities to help Scotland Yard. 1___

Rules of Engagement - 1989 - Murder and intrigue flourish when the town of Portsmouth is sealed off during WWIII. M___

Ruth Rendell Mysteries - 1987 to 2000 - While initial seasons of this anthology series focused on Rendell's CI Reg Wexford, later seasons merely focused on including elements of her stories. 1___ 2___ 3___ 4___ 5___ 6___ 7___ 8___ 9___ 10___ 11___ 12___

Safe - 2018 to present - American actor Michael C Hall (*Dexter*) stars in this series about a British widower whose daughter goes missing. 1___

Safe House - 2015 to 2017 – Christopher Eccleston (*Doctor Who*) stars in this series about a married couple asked to turn their guest house into a safe house. 1___ 2___

Sally Lockhart Mysteries - 2006 to 2007 - Two of the four Sally Lockhart novels were adapted into two television movies starring Billie Piper. M___

Save Me - 2018 to present - A man's life is turned upside-down when he suddenly finds himself accused of kidnapping an estranged daughter he hasn't seen in ten years. 1___ 2___

Scott & Bailey - 2011 to 2016 - Two very different female police detectives enjoy a close friendship and productive partnership. 1___ 2___ 3___ 4___ 5___

Second Sight - 1999 to 2000 - Clive Owen stars in this series of television movies about DCI Ross Tanner, a detective whose eyesight is rapidly fading. 1___ 2___

Seekers - 1993 - When a woman's private investigator husband disappears, she discovers he had another wife. 1___

Sergeant Cork - 1963 to 1968 - Set in Victorian times, Sergeant Cork goes against the establishment and tries to make his investigations more scientific. 1___ 2___

Shades of Darkness - 1983 to 1986 - This anthology series specializes in classic ghost stories. 1___ 2___

Shadow of the Noose - 1989 - This late 80s miniseries focuses on the work of Edward Marshall Hall, a prominent Victorian barrister. 1___

Shadows - 1975 to 1978 - This cult classic was a horror anthology series for children. 1___ 2___ 3___

Shadows of Fear - 1970 to 1973 - This anthology series featured people in weird and terrifying situations. 1___

Shakespeare & Hathaway - 2018 to present - In beautiful Stratford-Upon-Avon, an unlikely pair of private investigators solves crimes together. 1___ 2___

She's Out - 1995 - After serving 9 years for murdering her husband, Dolly Rawlins gets out. She has big plans, as does everyone around her. M___

Sherlock - 2010 to 2017 - Benedict Cumberbatch stars in this modern take on the original Sir Arthur Conan Doyle stories. 1___ 2___ 3___ 4___

Sherlock Holmes - 1965 to 1968 - Nigel Stock and Peter Cushing star as Watson and Holmes in this version of the classic stories. 1___ 2___

Sherlock Holmes - 1984 to 1994 - Jeremy Brett and David Burke star in this set of Sherlock Holmes adventures. 1___ 2___ 3___ 4___ 5___ 6___ 7___

Shetland - 2013 to present - In the remote island community of Shetland, DI Jimmy Perez and his team investigate threats to the peace of their village. 1___ 2___ 3___ 4___

Shoestring - 1979 to 1980 - A radio phone-in detective solves mysteries in the West Country in this lighthearted mystery series. 1___ 2___

Silent Witness - 1996 to present - A team of pathologists investigates crimes based on evidence gleaned from autopsies. 1___ 2___ 3___ 4___ 5___ 6___ 7___ 8___ 9___ 10___ 11___ 12___ 13___ 14___ 15___ 16___ 17___ 18___ 19___ 20___ 21___ 22___

Sinbad - 2012 - When a young man accidentally kills someone in a fight, he's cursed and his life spins out of control. 1___

Single-Handed - 2007 to 2010 - *Ireland* - Jack Driscoll is transferred back to his hometown to take over the Garda Sergeant role his father left. 1___ 2___ 3___ 4___

Softly, Softly - 1966 to 1969 - In the mythical area of Wyvern, a Regional Crime Squad fights crime. 1___ 2___ 3___ 4___ 5___

Southcliffe - 2013 - Told from the perspective of a journalist, this series tells the story of a shooting in an English market town. 1___

Special Branch - 1969 to 1974 - This groundbreaking crime drama focused on an elite group of officers assigned to protect London from high-end threats. 1___ 2___ 3___ 4___

Spender - 1991 to 1993 - In this gritty police drama, a detective in Northeast England solves crimes a lot better than he solves his marital issues. 1___ 2___ 3___

Spotless - 2015 to 2017 - A crime scene cleaner in London finds trouble when his criminal brother involves him in organized crime. 1___

Spyder's Web - 1972 - Secret government agents use the film industry as cover, posing as documentary filmmakers while solving crimes too tough for the normal police. 1___

Stan Lee's Lucky Man - 2016 to 2018 - In this action-crime drama from Stan Lee, a down-on-his-luck investigator suddenly gains the power to control luck - at a cost. 1___ 2___ 3___

State of Play - 2003 - A government conspiracy surrounds the death of a young politician's mistress/assistant. M___

Stay Lucky - 1989 to 1993 - A small-time gangster escapes London and heads north, finding himself drawn into a woman's life in Leeds. 1___ 2___ 3___ 4___

Stonemouth - 2015 - A man returns to his small Scottish hometown in hopes of finding out the truth about his friend's murder. 1___

Strange - 2002 to 2003 - An ex-priest hunts demons and bad elements within the church. 1___

Strange Report - 1969 to 1970 - This cult classic focuses on Adam Strange, a criminologist who works on cases beyond the skills of normal police. 1___

Strangers - 2018 - John Simm (Life on Mars) stars as a man whose life is turned upside down when his wife dies in a car accident in Hong Kong. 1___

Strike aka C.B. Strike - 2017 to present - Based on the Robert Galbraith novels by JK Rowling, this series follows PI Cormoran Strike and his highly-competent, Yorkshire-born assistant Robin. 1___ 2___

Supernatural - 1977 - In order to gain entry into a secret society, prospective members must tell a sufficiently frightening story or face death. 1___

Supply & Demand - 1997 to 1998 - This crime drama features an elite team of detectives charged with investigating large-scale smugglers and importers. 1___ 2___

Survivors - 2008 to 2010 - A group of otherwise normal people survive a devastating outbreak. 1___ 2___

Suspects - 2014 to 2016 - Three Greater London detectives investigate serious crimes in this heavily improvised series. 1___ 2___ 3___ 4___ 5___

Taggart - 1985 to 2010 - Originally a miniseries titled Killer, this long-running

Scottish police procedural features investigations of gruesome crimes in Glasgow (later expanding to other areas at times). 1__ 2__ 3__ 4__ 5__ 6__ 7__ 8__ 9__ 10__ 11__ 12__ 13__ 14__ 15__ 16__ 17__ 18__ 19__ 20__ 21__ 22__ 23__ 24__ 25__ 26__ 27__

Tales of the Unexpected - 1979 to 1988 - The short stories of Roald Dahl are dramatized in this series. 1__ 2__ 3__ 4__ 5__ 6__ 7__ 8__ 9__

Talking to the Dead - 2013 - A promising young DC with Cardiff Major Crimes attempts to solve a murder while dealing with Cotard's Syndrome. M__

Tatau - 2015 - This eight-part miniseries is a supernatural murder mystery set in the Cook Islands. M__

TECX - 1990 - This short-lived series featured 3 ambitious Belgian private investigators who took on cases around Britain, Holland, France, and Belgium. 1__ 2__

The ABC Murders - 2018 - John Malkovich stars as Poirot as he faces a mysterious serial killer known only as ABC. M__

The Adventures of Shirley Holmes - 1996 to 2000 - *Canada* - Sherlock Holmes's great-niece lives in Canada and solves crimes with her boyfriend. 1__ 2__ 3__ 4__

The Aphrodite Inheritance - 1979 - When a British engineer is involved in an accident in Greece, his brother flies out to find him dead. He quickly learns his brother was mixed up with some very strange people. M__

The Avengers - 1961 to 1969 - Suave spy John Steed works for British Intelligence and works on edgy cases where he saves the world repeatedly. 1__ 2__ 3__ 4__ 5__ 6__ 7__

The Baron - 1966 to 1967 - American actor Steve Forrest plays the role of an antiques dealer and undercover agent for British Diplomatic Intelligence. 1__

The Bay - 2019 to present - Morven Christie (Grantchester) plays DS Lisa Armstrong, a family liaison officer who discovers she has a personal connection to a missing persons case. 1__

The Bill - 1984 to 2010 - Daily life and crime around the Sun Hill Police Station is never easy. 1__ 2__ 3__ 4__ 5__ 6__ 7__ 8__ 9__ 10__ 11__ 12__ 13__ 14__ 15__ 16__ 17__ 18__ 19__ 20__ 21__ 22__ 23__ 24__ 25__ 26__

The Blackheath Poisonings - 1992 to 1993 - When a young man looks into the death of his father, it brings trouble between two families. M__

The Bletchley Circle - 2012 to 2014 - In 1952, four codebreakers from WWII come together to track a killer. 1__ 2__

The Bletchley Circle San Francisco - 2018 to present - Female code breakers from England solve murders in San Francisco. 1__

The Body Farm - 2011 - This police procedural focuses on a team at a forensic pathology research facility. 1__

The Brokenwood Mysteries - 2014 to 2017 - *New Zealand* - After a case takes him to the fictional town of Brokenwood, New Zealand, DI Mike Shepard reassesses his life and decides to stay in the small town indefinitely. 1___ 2___ 3___ 4___

The Broker's Man - 1997 to 1998 - An ex-cop now works for insurance companies. 1___ 2___

The Capture - 2019 to present - Holliday Grainger (*CB Strike*) stars in this series about a man fighting against flawed video surveillance to prove his innocence. 1___

The Champions - 1968 to 1969 - Agents for an international intelligence agency crash in the Himalayas and come out of it with super powers. 1___

The Chief - 1990 to 1995 - This critically-acclaimed series shows turmoil in an East Anglian police force after a woman is promoted to a deputy position. 1___ 2___ 3___ 4___ 5___

The City & the City - 2018 to present - Inspector Borlu investigates a murder in the twin city, which occupies the same space differently. 1___

The Clifton House Mystery - 1978 - When a family moves into an old home in Bristol, they discover a secret room with a skeleton and hire a ghost hunter to get rid of the spirits. 1___

The Coroner - 2015 to 2016 - A solicitor returns to her coastal hometown, becomes coroner, and investigates suspicious deaths. 1___ 2___

The Corridor People - 1966 to 1966 - This short-lived cult classic features a bizarre cast of characters up against the evil schemes of a Persian millionairess. 1___

The Dark Side of the Sun - 1983 - A British photographer is killed on assignment in Greece, and when his wife goes to investigate, she's drawn into sinister happenings. 1___

The Demon Headmaster - 1996 to 1998 - When a young girl moves in with a new foster family and starts at a new school, she notices something very strange going on. 1___ 2___ 3___ | CBBC Pantomime Special___

The Disappearance - 2015 - *France* - When a teenage girl disappears from a festival, dark secrets come to the surface. M___

The Disappearance - 2017 - *Canada* - When a boy disappears from his 10th birthday party, long-held family secrets begin to come out. M___

The Driver - 2014 - Life changes when a taxi driver agrees to drive for a criminal organization. M___

The Enfield Haunting - 2015 - In 1977, strange and terrifying things happen in a North London house. M___

The Expert - 1968 to 1976 - Professor John Hardy uses his forensic expertise to help the police. Parts of this series were lost. 1___ 2___ 3___ 4___

The Fades - 2011 - A young man who can see the spirits of the dead finds he's not alone, and the spirits are not harmless. 1___

Inspector Lynley stars Nathaniel Parker and Sharon Small have backgrounds that mirror their characters: Parker is the son of a knight, and Small was raised by a working-class single mother in Glasgow.

The Fall - 2013 to 2016 – Gillian Anderson (*The X-Files*) and Jamie Dornan (*50 Shades of Grey*) star in this Northern Ireland-based series about a cold serial killer facing off against an equally cold detective. 1___ 2___ 3___

The Fear - 1988 - A brutally-efficient London gangster pursues money and status with no regard for anyone else. 1___

The Fellows - 1967 - A former investigator, his partner, and a programmer investigate the changing nature of crime. 1___

The Field of Blood - 2011 to 2013 - In the early 1980s, a young woman skillfully solves murders on a police force full of men. 1___ 2___

The Five - 2016 - Twenty years after a young boy goes missing, his DNA turns up at a crime scene. 1___

The Four Just Men - 1959 to 1960 - Judi Dench makes an early appearance in this glamourous crime drama about four men summoned to Foxgrove Manor to hear a recording that implores them to band together and fight injustice. 1___

The Fourth Floor - 1986 - Two detectives from Scotland Yard's famed fourth floor investigate a complicated crime and attempt to prevent an even bigger one. M___

The Frankenstein Chronicles - 2015 to 2017 - Sean Bean stars in this period crime drama about an officer who discovers a corpse made up of body parts from missing children. 1___ 2___

The Frankie Drake Mysteries - 2017 to present - Frankie and her pal Trudy are the only female detectives in 1920s Toronto, and they're very good at what they do. 1___ 2___

The Frighteners - 1972 to 1973 - This anthology series features tales of horror with a number of major British television stars like John Thaw and Clive Swift. 1___

The Gentle Touch - 1980 to 1984 - Jill Gascoine stars as a single mother and firm but compassionate officer in what was the first series to show a woman at the DI level. 1___ 2___ 3___ 4___ 5___

The Ghosts of Motley Hall - 1976 to 1978 - This 20-episode 1970s children's series is about a deserted mansion populated by five argumentative ghosts. 1___ 2___ 3___ | 1977 Christmas Special___

The Gil Mayo Mysteries - 2006 - A charismatic detective and single father wisecracks his way through cases while hiding real pain about his past. 1___

The Gold Robbers - 1969 - A talented DCS attempts to hunt down those responsible for a massive gold robbery. 1___

The Great Train Robbery - 2013 - This miniseries examines the robbery first from the side of the robbers, and then from the side of the lawmen. M___

The Guilty - 2013 - This drama follows the aftermath of a 4-year-old boy's disappearance at a local barbecue. 1___

The Hanged Man - 1975 - After several attempts on his life, a businessman decides to stay dead until he figures out what's going on. 1___

The Helen West Casebook aka Helen West - 1999 to 2002 - Helen West is a workaholic crown prosecutor with a strong sense of justice and a messy personal life. 1___

The Honourable Woman - 2014 - Maggie Gyllenhaal stars in this political spy thriller about an Anglo-Jewish woman who inherits her father's arms business and works towards Palestine-Israeli reconciliation. M___

The Hour - 2011 to 2012 - This Cold War-era thriller focuses on three employees at an investigative news program. 1___ 2___

The Ice Cream Girls - 2013 - Based on the Dorothy Koomson novel, this series follows two vulnerable young girls accused of murdering their teacher. M___

The Ice House - 1997 - The peaceful lives of three women are shattered when a corpse is discovered in the ice house on their property. M___

The Innocence Project - 2006 to 2007 - A law professor and his students seek out cases where justice has not been served. Then tirelessly work to correct it. 1___

The Innocents - 2018 to present - This supernatural series follows two teenagers as they run away together, later discovering that one of them has shape-shifting abilities. 1___

The Inspector Alleyn Mysteries - 1990 to 1994 - This entertaining period mystery features clever crimes and clever-er solutions. 1___ 2___

The Inspector Lynley Mysteries - 2001 to 2008 - An Oxford-educated detective pairs up with a working-class partner to investigate mysteries. 1___ 2___ 3___ 4___ 5___ 6___

The Jury - 2002 to 2011 - A jury is called up for the retrial of a triple murder suspect. 1___ 2___

The Knock - 1994 to 2000 - This series follows Customs and Excise officers as they attempt to hunt down smugglers and contraband. 1___ 2___ 3___ 4___ 5___

The Last Detective - 2003 to 2007 - Because he's decent, old fashioned and a generally good guy, his fellow detectives and his boss don't like him much. Still, DC Davies proves that his style works by constantly solving cases no one else wants. 1___ 2___ 3___ 4___

The Last Honour of Christopher Jeffries - 2014 - This miniseries tells the story of when retired schoolteacher and landlord Christopher Jeffries was accused of involvement in a tenant's murder. M___

The Last Panthers - 2015 - This series focuses on a gang of high-end thieves closely resembling the Balkan jewel thieves known as the Pink Panthers. 1__

The Last Weekend - 2012 - Old university friends get together for a reunion, but their competitive natures cause problems that grow with each passing day. 1__

The Level - 2016 to 2017 - A detective is the missing witness in the murder of a drug trafficker. The police want her, and the killer wants her dead. 1__

The Living and the Dead - 2016 - Supernatural forces threaten a young couple on a farm they have inherited. M__

The Loch aka Loch Ness - 2017 to present - Highlands Detective Annie Redford faces her first murder case when a human heart is found. 1__

The Long Firm - 2004 - In the dark underbelly of 1960s London, gangster and porn king Harry Starks is both ruthless and sensitive, with an enduring love of Judy Garland. M__

The Mad Death - 1983 - This frightening series looks at a rabies outbreak in Britain. M__

The Man in Room 17 - 1965 to 1966 - In a secret government department called Room 17, two men solve crimes without ever leaving the office. 1__ 2__

The Mind of Mr. JG Reeder - 1969 to 1971 - Based on the short stories of Edgar Wallace, a shabby detective uses his brilliant criminal mind to solve cases. 1__ 2__

The Missing - 2014 to 2016 - Retired French detective Julien Baptiste solves difficult missing persons cases. 1__ 2__

The Moonstone - 2016 - Based on what is widely considered the first detective novel, this series tells the story of a missing diamond at an English country house. M__

The Moorside - 2017 - This miniseries follows the search for a missing Yorkshire schoolgirl. M__

The Mystery of Edwin Drood - 2012 - This miniseries is an adaptation of Charles Dickens's tale of the death of Edwin Drood. M__

The Mystery of Lord Lucan aka Lucan - 2013 – Accused of murdering his children's nanny, Lord Lucan would disappear soon after. M__

The Night Manager - 2016 to present - The night manager of a Cairo hotel is recruited to work as a spy. 1__ 2__

The Nightmare World of H.G. Wells - 2016 - This four-part series explores several lesser-known short stories by H.G. Wells. M__

The No. 1 Ladies Detective Agency - 2008 to 2009 - When her father dies, Precious sells the farm and opens a detective agency with Grace. 1__

The Protectors - 1972 to 1974 - Three elite "freelance troubleshooters" fight crime around the world. 1__ 2__

The Reckoning - 2011 - Ashley Jensen stars alongside Max Beesley as a single

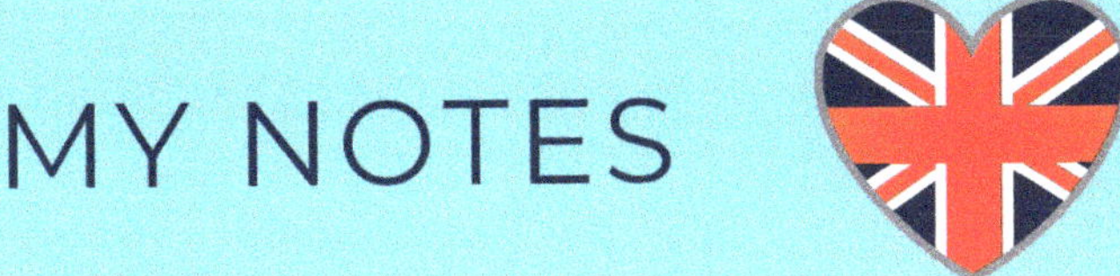
MY NOTES

mother who's been offered a large sum of money on the condition that she kill a man. M___

The Replacement - 2017 - When a woman prepares to begin maternity leave, she realizes her replacement may be trying to take over her entire life. M___

The Rivals of Sherlock Holmes - 1971 to 1973 - This series features mysteries about detectives other than Holmes, but written around the same time period. 1___ 2___

The Runaway - 2011 - This gritty period crime drama is set in 60s and 70s London and focuses on the doomed romance of two childhood friends. 1___

The Ruth Rendell Mysteries - 1987 to 2000 - This series features mysteries based on Ruth Rendell's Detective Inspector Wexford stories. 1___ 2___ 3___ 4___ 5___ 6___ 7___ 8___ 9___ 10___ 11___ 12___

The Sally Lockhart Mysteries - 2006 to 2007 - This series was made up of 2 TV movies: *The Shadow in the North* and *The Ruby in the Smoke*. 1___

The Sandbaggers - 1978 to 1980 - This series focuses on the missions of an elite British Intelligence group specializing in covert operations. 1___ 2___ 3___

The Secret - 2016 - James Nesbitt (*Cold Feet*) stars as killer dentist Colin Howell in this adaptation of a true story. M___

The Secret Agent - 2016 - In Victorian England, Toby Jones (*Detectorists*) stars as a sex shop owner and foreign spy. M___

The Secret of Crickley Hall - 2012 - Not long after the disappearance of her son, Eve and her family move to Crickley Hall and supernatural events begin to occur. Stars Suranne Jones (*Scott & Bailey*) and Tom Ellis (*Miranda*). M___

The Shadow Line - 2011 - DI Gabriel investigates the killing of a drug baron while one of the drug baron's former associates conducts his own investigation. M___

The Silence - 2010 - A hearing impaired 18-year-old witnesses the murder of a police officer. M___

The Singing Detective - 1986 - Michael Gambon plays a desperately ill writer reliving his detective stories through a cloud of hallucination and imagination. M___

The Suspicions of Mr. Whicher - 2011 to 2014 - This series of DI Jack Whicher films is made up of The Murder at Road Hill House, The Murder in Angel Lane, Beyond the Pale, and The Ties that Bind. M___

The Sweeney - 1975 to 1978 - John Thaw and Dennis Waterman star in this 1970s series about police tackling violent crimes in London. 1___ 2___ 3___ 4___

The Take - 2009 - Tom Hardy and Shaun Evans star in this series about two brothers, one freshly out of prison, as they move through organized crime circles. M___

The Tomorrow People - 1973 to 1979 - This cult classic is about a group of British teens with special powers that include telepathy and teleportation. 1___ 2___ 3___ 4___ 5___ 6___ 7___ 8___

Mystery writer Ruth Rendell was once forced to resign from a local paper after turning in a story about an event she hadn't attended - because she failed to report that one of the speakers had died during his speech.

The Top-Secret Life of Edgar Briggs - 1974 - Bumbling Edgar Briggs solves cases for the British Intelligence Service in spite of himself. 1___

The Trial of Christine Keeler - 2019 - This upcoming BBC One political drama is based on the 1960s Profumo Scandal. 1___

The Trials of Jimmy Rose - 2015 - A man tries to go straight after getting out of prison, but finds his personal life in shambles. 1___

The Tunnel - 2013 to present - This British-French crime drama features investigations of crimes that occur between the two countries. 1✓ 2✓ 3✓

The Vice - 1999 to 2003 - Ken Stott and Caroline Catz are among the main characters in this series about a London vice squad. 1___ 2___ 3___ 4___ 5___

The War of the Worlds - 2019 - In Edwardian London, a young couple's new life together is disrupted by a Martian invasion. M___

The Whistleblowers - 2007 - Two young lawyers help find justice for victims of government and corporate corruption. 1___

The Widower - 2014 - This three-part miniseries is based on the true story of a man who attempted to kill a number of women with whom he was romantically involved. M✓

The Wimbledon Poisoner - 1994 - A boring solicitor is tired of his bullying wife, so he decides to murder her. 1___

The Witness for the Prosecution - 2016 to 2017 - When a wealthy heiress is murdered, investigators have to determine who's telling the truth. 1___

The Worricker Trilogy - 2014 - An analyst in the British intelligence forces want to find out why the PM had his friend killed. 1___

The XYY Man - 1976 to 1977 - A cat burglar is hired by British intelligence services in hopes of putting his skills to good use. 1___ 2___

Thief Takers - 1995 to 1997 - This series focuses on the personal and professional lives of police officers who specialize in handling armed robberies. 1___ 2___ 3___

Thirteen - 2016 - After 13 years of being held captive, Ivy Moxam steps out onto the street. 1___

Thirteen Against Fate - 1966 - This mystery series features thirteen standalone stories by Georges SImenon, creator of the Maigret series. 1___

Thirteen Steps Down - 2012 - A man stalks a supermodel and moves deeper into his obsession with a serial killer. 1___

Thorne - 2010 - DI Thorne investigates a

serial killer who has manipulated one of his victims into a stroke, unable to communicate but aware of everything. 1___

Thriller - 1973 to 1976 - This 1970s horror anthology program ranges from supernatural stories to psychological thrillers. 1___ 2___ 3___ 4___ 5___ 6___

Timeslip - 1970 to 1971 - Two young friends find a time barrier that allows them to travel to different time periods, often finding themselves caught up in strange adventures. 1___

Tin Star - 2017 to present - Set in a sleepy Canadian town, Tim Roth plays a New Chief of Police who has to deal with the violence and crime that follows big money into town. 1___ 2___

Top Boy - 2011 to 2013 - Top Boy follows the plight of a young man in a Hackney housing estate after his mother is committed for mental health issues. 1___ 2___

Torchwood - 2006 to 2011 - A secret agency called Torchwood fights off threats from aliens and the supernatural. 1___ 2___ 3___ 4___

Touching Evil - 1997 to 1999 - Robson Green and Nicola Walker star in this crime drama about the Organised & Serial Crime Unit. 1___ 2___ 3___

Travelling Man - 1984 to 1985 - After doing time for a bribe he never accepted, ex-DI Alan Lomax takes to a canal boat to exact his revenge. 1___ 2___

Trial and Retribution - 1997 to 2009 - DS Walker and his team follow criminals from their crime to the courts. 1___ 2___ 3___ 4___

5___ 6___ 7___ 8___ 9___ 10___ 11___ 12___

True Dare Kiss - 2007 - Four sisters come together after their father's death, and old secrets bubble to the surface. 1___

Trust Me - 2017 to present - When a whistleblowing nurse loses her job, she must find a way to take care of her daughter. 1___ 2___

Undeniable - 2014 - As a child, Jane Phillips saw a man murder her mother. As an adult, she believes she's seen that man, but almost no one believes her. 1___

Undercover - 2016 - When a lawyer takes a job as the first black Director of Public Prosecutions, she discovers her husband may not be who she thinks he is. 1___

Undermind - 1965 - An alien force uses high frequency signals to brainwash people into doing subversive acts, in preparation for a full invasion. 1___

Unforgotten - 2017 to present - A pair of London detectives work together to solve historic cold cases. 1✓ 2✓ 3✓ 4✓

Utopia - 2013 to 2014 - This thriller follows a group of people in possession of a graphic novel said to have predicted the worst disasters in human history. 1___ 2___

Vera - 2011 to present - DCI Vera Stanhope investigates murders in the Northumberland countryside. 1✓ 2✓ 3✓ 4✓ 5✓ 6✓ 7✓ 8✓ 9✓

Vexed - 2010 to 2012 - Detectives Jack and Georgina have a certain chemistry, but it's complicated. 1___ 2___

Villains - 1972 - This series looks at the criminal misadventures of nine bank robbers. 1___

Vincent - 2005 to 2006 - Vincent is an ex-cop who becomes a private investigator and takes on the tough cases. 1___ 2___

Waking the Dead - 2000 to 2011 - Using new technology, DS Boyd and his team open unsolved cases. 1___ 2___ 3___ 4___ 5___ 6___ 7___ 8___ 9___

Wallander - 2008 to 2016 - This English-language, Sweden-based mystery series is an adaptation of Henning Mankell's novels about Kurt Wallander, a highly empathetic detective. 1___ 2___ 3___

What Remains - 2013 - When a young couple moves into an apartment, they find a dead body and it kicks off an investigation into a young woman's disappearance two years prior. 1___

Whitechapel - 2009 to 2013 - An inspector, a detective sergeant, and a historical homicide expert look at crimes that may have connections to the Whitechapel district. 1✓ 2✓ 3✓ 4✓

Whodunnit - 2013 - Thirteen contestants try to follow the clues and figure who committed the murder. 1___

Wilde Alliance - 1978 - This series follows the investigative efforts of husband and wife amateur detectives, Rupert and Amy Wilde. 1___

Winter - 2015 - *Australia* - Eve Winter, a Sydney homicide detective, solves some of the most difficult cases while dealing with bureaucracy and the challenges of being a woman in her field. 1___

Wire in the Blood - 2002 to 2009 - An eccentric psychologist helps the police solve murders by getting inside the minds of the killers. 1___ 2___ 3___ 4___ 5___ 6___

Without Motive - 2000 to 2001 - A detective attempts to solve a series of murders that seemingly lack motive. 1___ 2___

WPC 56 - 2013 to 2015 - This period drama dives into the challenges faced by the first WPC (Woman Police Constable) in a West Midlands police force in the 1950s. 1___ 2___ 3___

Wycliffe - 1994 to 1998 – Based on W.J. Burley's novels, this Cornwall-based series features DS Charles Wycliffe, a man who investigates murders with a unique level of determination and accuracy. 1___ 2___ 3___ 4___ 5___

Z Cars - 1962 to 1978 - Of the 801 episodes made of this gritty Lancashire-based police drama, fewer than half survive. 1___ 2___ 3___ 4___ 5___ 6___ 7___ 8___ 9___ 10___ 11___ 12___

Zastrozzi - 1986 - This retelling of Mary Shelley's Frankenstein puts the characters into present-day England. M___

Zen - 2011 - A handsome detective works to bring integrity and justice to Roman streets. 1___

Zodiac - 1974 - A logical cop meets a pretty young astrologer and finds his ideas about the world tested. 1___

40 - 2003 - As an ad executive approaches 40, he realizes he's been left out of his class reunion and it sets him off on a journey. M__

1990 - 1977 to 1978 - In the future of Britain, a tyrannical government disregards the civil liberties of its citizens. 1__ 2__

19-2 - 2014 to present - *Canada* - This character-driven drama focuses on the lives of first responders at the Montreal Police Department. 1__ 2__ 3__ 4__

32 Brinkburn Street - 2011 - This drama looks at the lives of two generations of a family at one address, one in 1931 and the other in 2011. M__

37 Days - 2014 – This series zeroes in on the hidden events that occurred in the final days before the outbreak of WWI. M__

800 Words - 2015 to 2018 - *Australia* - After the death of his wife, a man relocates his family from Sydney to a small coastal community in New Zealand. 1✓ 2✓ 3✓

A Dance to the Music of Time - 1997 - This adaptation of Anthony Powell's novel of the same name charts the lives of characters from the 1920s thru the 1960s. M__

A Discovery of Witches - 2018 to present - A historian and reluctant witch attempts to decipher a mysterious manuscript from Oxford's Bodleian Library. 1__

A for Andromeda - 1961 - Scientists detect a radio signal from another galaxy, then follow its instructions. 1__

A Horseman Riding By - 1978 - After a war injury, a young man buys a neglected Devon estate with money from his father, and must then face locals who think he's not up to the job. 1__

A Little Princess - 1987 - A wealthy young girl is forced into servitude when her father loses his money and dies. M__

A Passionate Woman - 2010 - A bored 1950s mother falls in mad, passionate love with a neighbour and her life is changed forever. M__

A Perfect Hero - 1991 - Nigel Havers stars as an officer shot down and badly burned during the Battle of Britain. 1__

A Perfect Spy - 1987 - Based on the John Le Carre novel of the same name, this miniseries tells the story of a spy over the course of his life. M__

A Place to Call Home - 2013 to 2018 - *Australia* - A mysterious woman begins a new life in Australia after World War II. 1✓ 2✓ 3✓ 4✓ 5✓ 6✓

A Tale of Two Cities - 1989 - Set against the backdrop of the French Revolution, two men fall in love with the same woman. M___

A Tale of Two Cities - 1980 - This miniseries is based on the Dickens novel of the same name, telling the story of two men in love with the same woman. M___

A Very British Coup - 1988 - This miniseries tells the story of Harry Perkins, steel worker and eventual Prime Minister. M___

A Very English Scandal - 2018 - Hugh Grant plays a Liberal Party leader who was tried for conspiring to kill his homosexual lover in 1979. M___

A Woman of Substance - 1984 - Emma Harte starts life as a kitchen maid, but heads up a manufacturing empire by the time WWII breaks out. M___

A Woman's Guide to Adultery - 1993 - This series tells the stories of three women involved in affairs. M___

A Year in Provence - 1993 - John Thaw stars in this series about a couple who leave their jobs for the South of France, only to meet with comical disasters at every turn. M___

A Young Doctor's Notebook - 2012 to 2013 - In the early 1900s, a young doctor comes to a Russian village to help out an older doctor at a local hospital. 1___ 2___

Ackley Bridge - 2017 to present - Two struggling schools merge to form one, and it creates big problems for the headmistress. 1___ 2___

Age Before Beauty - 2018 to present - This contemporary drama is set in a struggling family-owned beauty salon in Manchester. 1___

All Creatures Great & Small - 1978 to 1990 - Veterinarian James Herriot begins his career in 1940s Yorkshire. 1___ 2___ 3___ 4___ 5___ 6___ 7___ | Christmas Specials: 1983___ 1985___ 1990___

All Passion Spent - 1986 - After her politician husband dies, Lady Slane moves to the countryside in search of her own identity. 1___

All thc Small Things - 2009 - A choirmaster develops a crush on a new member and leaves his wife and kids. 1___

Alys - 2011 to 2012 - After trouble in Cardiff, a woman moves herself and her son to a small village in rural Wales. 1___ 2___

An Age of Kings - 1960 to 1961 - This series links Shakespeare's Richard II and Richard III, filling in the gaps with the history that came in between them. 1___

Anglo-Saxon Attitudes - 1992 - This dramatic satire sees an aging historian come to terms with the events of his life. M___

Anna Karenina - 2000 to 2001 - Helen McCrory plays the title role in this adaptation of Tolstoy's classic novel. M___

Annie's Bar - 1996 - This satirical political drama is set in the world of a newly-elected conservative MP. 1__

Any Human Heart - 2010 - A novelist's life bounces around in space and time, causing him to meet up with a number of famous historic figures. M__

Anzac Girls - 2014 - Heroic women rise to the occasion during the war. M__

Apparitions - 2008 - Father Jacob verifies evidence of miracles and does exorcisms. M__

Apple Tree Yard - 2017 to present - A married woman with two grown children has an affair that changes her formerly conventional life. 1__

Aristocrats - 1999 - This miniseries follows the lives of four aristocratic sisters through 1700s England. M__

Armchair Theatre - 1956 to 1974 - This drama anthology series features individual plays addressing timeless human issues. 1__ 2__ 3__ 4__ 5__ 6__ 7__ 8__ 9__ 10__ 11__ 12__ 13__ 14__ 15__ 16__

As If - 2001 to 2004 - This comedy-drama series focuses on the lives and loves of a group of teenagers in early 21st-century London. 1__ 2__ 3__ 4__

Ashenden - 1991 - A writer is recruited to be a spy in WWI. M__

At Home with the Braithwaites - 2000 to 2003 - When a normal family wins the lottery, it changes their lives. 1__ 2__ 3__ 4__

Atlantis - 2013 to 2017 - Jason mysteriously disappears from the present and lands on the shores of ancient Atlantis. 1__ 2__

Babyfather - 2001 to 2002 - Four men living in London deal with secrets, infidelity, and pregnancies. 1__ 2__

Baker Boys - 2011 - After the local bakery that employs them goes broke, the staff decides to take it over. 1__ 2__

Ballykissangel - 1996 to 2001 - *Ireland* - A young English priest adjusts to the pace of life in a small Irish village. 1__ 2__ 3__ 4__ 5__ 6__

Banana - 2015 - This series explores the relationships of 8 different couples as they come to terms with love. M__

Banished - 2015 - When British convicts are sent to Australia to pay for their crimes, they and the soldiers who guard them have to adapt to the new world. M__

Barchester Chronicles - 1982 - This miniseries is an adaptation of Anthony Trollope's first two novels in the Chronicles of Barsetshire series. M__

Beau Geste - 1982 - Three well-off English brothers join the French Foreign Legion. M__

Bed of Roses - 2008 to 2011 - *Australia* - A mother and daughter struggle after the death of their husband and father. 1__ 2__ 3__

Beecham House - 2019 to present - This period drama takes place in Delhi in 1795, focusing on a British family attempting to establish a life there before British rule. 1__

Behaving Badly - 1989 - Dame Judi Dench

stars in this funny drama about a woman who decides not to take things lying down after her husband leaves her for a much younger woman. M___

Being Human - 2008 to 2013 - A werewolf, vampire, and ghost live as roommates in modern-day England. 1___ 2___ 3___ 4___ 5___

Beowolf: Return to the Shieldlands - 2016 - When Beowulf returns to his homeland, he is unwelcome, especially with his family. M___

Berkeley Square - 1998 - Three women from varied backgrounds get jobs working for the wealthy families of Berkeley Square. M___

Between the Sheets - 2003 - Hazel has a loveless marriage until she has an affair with a younger man and has her first orgasm. M___

Bird of Prey - 1982 - An international criminal organization feels the heat from a small-time bureaucrat. M___

Bird of Prey 2 - 1984 - In this sequel to *Bird of Prey*, the criminals turn the tables and come after bank clerk Henry Jay. M___

Birdsong - 2012 - In WWI, a British soldier fights in the trenches of France and dreams of a forbidden love affair. 1___

Black Mirror - 2011 to present - This anthology series showcases the perils of technological advancement. 1___ 2___ 3___ 4___ 5___

Blackpool - 2004 - Shortly after Ripley Holden opens his arcade, a man is murdered. The investigation jeopardizes all his big plans. 1___ | Viva Blackpool TV Movie ___

Bleak House - 2005 - This classic BBC adaptation is based on the Dickens legal drama of the same name. M___

Bluebell - 1986 - This series tells the true story of Margaret Kelly, a woman who founded a famous dance troupe in Paris. 1___

Bodies - 2004 to 2006 - This graphic medical drama features a young doctor who begins a new gynaecology post. 1___ 2___ | Feature-length Finale ___

Bodyguard - 2018 to present - This thriller focuses on a former soldier assigned to protect the Home Secretary. 1___

Bombshell - 2006 - In spite of a cast that included Bertie Carvel and Zöe Lucker, this series about life in the British Army never actually aired in the UK. 1___

Bonekickers - 2008 - Hugh Bonneville stars in this series about a team that handles high-profile antiquities finds. 1___

Born & Bred - 2001 to 2005 - This series follows the lives of a father and son doctor team in the 1950s. 1___ 2___ 3___ 4___ | 2003 Christmas Special___

Bouquet of Barbed Wire - 1976 - Scandalous when released, this series that looks at the sexual tensions in a seemingly normal family in the English middle class during the 70s. M___

Bouquet of Barbed Wire - 2010 - This modern version of the 70s miniseries included Trevor Eve (*Waking the Dead*) and Hermione Norris (*Cold Feet*). M___

Bramwell - 1995 to 1998 - Set in 1895, Eleanor Bramwell works first under a doctor's supervision and then opens her own infirmary. 1✓ 2✓ 3✓ 4✓

Breathless - 2013 - Set in early 1960s England, this series looks at the lives of hospital staff who perform illegal off-site abortions in their spare time. 1___

Breeze Block - 2002 - After being made redundant, a Newcastle man struggles to regain his confidence. 1___

Brief Encounters - 2016 - When a group of women start selling lingerie and other marital aids through at-home parties in the early 1980s, their lives are transformed. 1___

Brittania - 2018 to present - This series is set in AD 43 and follows the Roman conquest of Britain. 1___

Broken - 2017 to present - Sean Bean stars as Father Michael, a flawed but good-hearted Catholic priest in Northern England. 1✓

Bugs - 1995 to 1999 - Beckett leaves a secret intelligence agency and starts his own group of agents to fight high-tech crimes. 1___ 2___ 3___ 4___

Bulletproof - 2018 to present - This series follows detectives at the National Crime Agency as they deal with some of the UK's most dangerous criminals. 1___ 2___

Buried - 2003 - This BBC drama offers a gritty portrayal of an innocent man's life in a British prison. 1___

Butterfly - 2018 - This series focuses on a couple coming to terms with their child's gender transition. M___

By the Sword Divided - 1983 to 1985 - This period drama tells the story of the English Civil War through the eyes of two families, one on each side of the conflict. 1___ 2___

Byker Grove - 1989 to 2006 - This series looks at the daily lives of kids in a youth club. 1___ 2___ 3___ 4___ 5___ 6___ 7___ 8___ 9___ 10___ 11___ 12___ 13___ 14___ 15___ 16___ 17___ 18___

Call the Midwife - 2012 to present - This international hit focuses on a group of East London midwives in the 1950s and 60s. 1___ 2___ 3___ 4___ 5___ 6___ 7___ 8___ 9___ | Christmas Specials: 12___ 13___ 14___ 15___ 16___ 17___ 18___

Cambridge Spies - 2003 - This miniseries is based on the true story of Cambridge students recruited to spy for the Soviet Union in the 1930s. M___

Camelot - 2011 - After the death of King

Uther and impending chaos, Merlin presents a young unknown as the new king. 1___

Capital - 2015 - When property values soar on a once middle-class London street, residents receive mysterious postcards saying, "We want what you have." M___

Capstick's Law - 1989 - This period drama focuses on a firm of Yorkshire-based solicitors in the 1950s. 1___

Casanova - 1971 - Casanova's imprisonment is contrasted with his sensual escapades. M___

Casanova - 2005 - This miniseries looks at the Casanova story from the perspective of his much older self. M___

Casualty 1900s – 2006 to 2009 – This series tells tales of a historic London hospital thru the records and diaries of nurses who worked there. Casualty 1906___ Casualty 1907___ Casualty 1909___

Children of the Stones - 1977 - A man and his son move to a sleepy English village and find something mysterious controlling the local residents. 1___

Christabel - 1988 - A young Englishwoman marries a German man and attempts to live a normal life in 1930s Germany. M___

Cilla - 2014 - Cilla tells the story of British entertainer Cilla Black and her rise to fame in 1960s Liverpool. M___

Claire - 1982 - A middle-class British family takes in a teenage foster child and gets more chaos than they bargained for. 1___

Clayhanger - 1976 - In 19th century England, Edwin Clayhanger wants to be an architect, but his family wants him to continue in their printing business. 1___

Cleverman - 2016 to 2017 - *Australia* - In a dystopian future, ancient mythological creatures live among humans. 1___ 2___

Clique - 2017 to present - Two friends go off to university in Edinburgh, but one is pulled away into a dark and seductive clique. 1___ 2___

Clocking Off - 2000 to 2003 – This drama zeroes in on the interconnected lives of different employees in a Manchester textile factory. 1___ 2___ 3___ 4___

Close & True - 2000 - In Newcastle, an inexperienced solicitor takes over operations of a poorly-run legal practice. 1___

Close to the Enemy - 2016 - After WW2, a German engineer is taken to Britain in hopes of gaining his cooperation. M___

Colour Blind - 1998 - This three-episode miniseries features a WWI-era family turned upside-down by an interracial marriage. M___

Coming Up - 2003 to 2013 - Each series of this anthology show features eight episodes by writers and directors with little to no experience. 1___ 2___ 3___ 4___ 5___ 6___ 7___ 8___ 9___ 10___ 11___

Conditions - 2019 to present - The retiring director of a home for challenged adults drives through and notices all hell has broken loose. 1___

Country Matters - 1973 to 1979 - Based on the short stories of A.E. Coppard and H.E.

Bates, this period drama is set in the post-WWI English countryside. 1__ 2__

Covington Cross - 1992 - This British-American series was set in 1300s England and followed widower Sir Thomas Grey and his family. 1__

Cranford - 2008 to 2010 - Cranford tells the story of women in a small, fictional market town at the dawn of the Industrial Revolution. Judi Dench stars in this modern remake of the 1972 miniseries. 1✓ 2✓

Cranford - 1972 - Cranford tells the story of women in a small, fictional market town at the dawn of the Industrial Revolution. M__

Crime & Punishment - 1979 - This miniseries is based on Dostoevsky's classic novel about crime and conscience. M__

Critical - 2015 - This medical drama is set in a fictional major trauma center. 1__

Crowdie & Cream - 2002 - Based on the memoirs of Finlay MacDonald, this series tells of life in the Scottish Hebrides Islands in the 1930s. M__

Crownies - 2011 - *Australia* - This Australian legal drama follows five young solicitors as they begin their careers. 1__

Cucumber - 2015 - This series offers a peek inside the lives of gay men in modern Manchester. M__

Curfew - 2019 to present - Sean Bean and Adrian Brody star in this series about illegal street races in Manchester. 1__

Cutting It - 2002 to 2005 - Hair professionals at the Henshall-Ferraday Hair Salon do battle in both their private and professional lives. 1__ 2__ 3__ 4__

Da Vinci's Demons - 2013 to 2015 - This series follows Leonardo Da Vinci as a young artist in Florence. 1__ 2__ 3__

Dancing on the Edge - 2013 - This period drama focuses on the experience of a black jazz band in 1930s London. 1__

Dandelion Dead - 1994 - A solicitor in the early 1920s is charged with the murder of his wife and attempted murder of a rival with arsenic. He says he bought the arsenic to kill dandelions. 1__

Danger Man - 1960 to 1962 - Secret agent John Drake deals with assignments that threaten world peace. 1__

Danger UXB - 1979 - Anthony Andrews stars as Lieutenant Brian Ash, a member of an unexploded bomb unit during WW2. 1__

Daniel Deronda - 1970 - Based on the novel by George Eliot, this miniseries focuses on kind Daniel Deronda and the beautiful but spoiled Gwendolen Harleth. M__

Daniel Deronda - 2002 - Gwendolen falls in love with nice man, but needs financial security he may not be able to offer. M✓

Dark Mon£y - 2019 - When their child is abused by a film producer, a family accepts hush money to stay silent. M__

Dates - 2013 to 2013 - Each episode of this romantic drama focuses on one first date in London. 1__

David Copperfield - 1974 to 1975 - This

production of the classic Dickens novel includes Dame Patricia Routledge (*Keeping Up Appearances*) as Mrs. Micawber. M___

David Copperfield - 1986 to 1986 - Based on the Dickens novel, a tender-hearted orphan makes his way in the world. M___

David Copperfield - 1999 - Daniel Radcliffe stars as young David in this adaptation of the Dickens novel. M___

Deadline Gallipoli - 2015 - Three journalists arrive in Gallipoli in 1915 to report on the war alongside British and Allied troops. M___

Dear Murderer - 2017 to present - *New Zealand* - This series tells the true story of Mike Bungay, one of New Zealand's most successful and controversial defense lawyers. 1___

Death & Nightingales - 2019 to present - Jamie Dornan stars in this period drama about love, deception, and revenge in the Fermanagh countryside in 1885 Northern Ireland. 1___

Decline & Fall - 2017 to present - After a prank, an Oxford student is wrongly dismissed for indecent exposure, going to work at a sub-par private school in Wales. 1___

Deep State - 2018 to present - This is the story of a man who does "one more job" for MI6. 1___

Delicious - 2016 to present - Two women in Cornwall try to get on somewhat peacefully after circumstances in their lives change dramatically. 1___ 2___ 3___

Desperate Romantics - 2009 - This period drama tells the story of the rise of the Pre-Raphaelite brotherhood. M___

Diana - 1984 - In 1920s England, a poor but promising country boy meets the daughter of a wealthy landowner. M___

Dickensian - 2015 to 2016 - Some of Charles Dickens's most memorable characters intertwine in 1800s London. 1___

Die Kinder - 1990 - Miranda Richardson stars in this series about a woman searching for her children after they're abducted by her ex-husband. M___

Disraeli - 1978 to 1980 - This miniseries follows the ups and downs in the life of famed politician Benjamin Disraeli. 1___

Doctor Finlay - 1993 to 1996 - After WW2 and before the NHS is created, a doctor returns to his Scottish hometown. 1___ 2___ 3___ 4___

Doctor Finlay's Casebook - 1962 to 1971 - In the late 1920s, Dr. Finlay practices medicine in a small Scottish town. 1___ 2___ 3___ 4___ 5___ 6___ 7___ 8___

Doctor Foster - 2015 to present - When a woman finds out her husband is having an affair, she goes a bit mad. 1___ 2___

Doctor Thorne - 2016 to present - A poor girl is raised by her uncle, Doctor Thorne. 1✓

Doctor Who - 1963 to present - A mysterious Time Lord travels through time and space, exploring and saving the world in equal measure. **Classic Doctor Who**: |**1st**

Doctor| 1__ 2__ 3__ |**2nd Doctor**| 4__ 5__ 6__ |**3rd Doctor**| 7__ 8__ 9__ 10__ 11__ |**4th Doctor**| 12__ 13__ 14__ 15__ 16__ 17__ 18__ |**5th Doctor**| 19__ 20__ 21__ |**6th Doctor**| 22__ 23__ |**7th Doctor**| 24__ 25__ 26__ |**8th Doctor**|TV Movie__ **Revived Doctor Who**: |**9th Doctor**| 1 __ |**10th Doctor**| 2__ 3__ 4__ The Next Doctor__ Planet of the Dead__ The Waters of Mars__ The End of Time, Part 1__ The End of Time, Part 2__ |**11th Doctor**| 5__ 6__ 7__ The Day of the Doctor__ The Time of the Doctor__ |**12th Doctor**| 8__ 9__ 10__ |**13th Doctor**| 11__

Dombey & Son - 1969 – This miniseries is an adaptation of a Charles Dickens story about a man who wants an heir for his business, only to lose his wife after she bears him a son. M__

Dominion Creek aka An Klondike - 2015 to present - *Ireland* - Three Irish brothers dream of striking it rich in the Klondike Gold Rush. 1__ 2__

Downton Abbey - 2010 to 2015 - This period drama follows the lives of the Crawley family and their servants during the early 1900s. 1✓ 2✓ 3✓ 4✓ 5✓ 6✓ | 2019 Movie__ ?

Drover's Gold - 1997 - Before the railroads, the British had to herd cattle across country to the markets. 1__

East of Everything - 2008 to 2009 - *Australia* - When an Australian woman dies, she dictates in her will that her two estranged sons must reopen the family hostel in Broken Bay. 1__ 2__

East West 101 - 2007 to 2011 - *Australia* - Detective Zane Malik investigates terror and other major crimes on the streets of Sydney. 1__ 2__ 3__

Edward & Mrs. Simpson - 1978 - This seven-part series is a dramatization of the events surrounding the abdication of King Edward VIII. M__

Edward the Seventh aka Edward the King - 1975 - This miniseries tells the story of Queen Victoria's son Edward VII - playboy, reformer, and elitist. M__

Elizabeth I - 2006 - Helen Mirren stars in this miniseries about the later years of Queen Elizabeth I. M__

Englistan - 2019 to present - This series tells the story of a British Pakistani family over several decades and generations. 1__

Fall of Eagles - 1974 - This miniseries charts the endings of three different European family dynasties. M__

Fallen Hero - 1978 to 1979 - After a career-ending rugby injury, a man works to rebuild his life. 1__ 2__

Fanny Hill - 2007 - Based on the scandalous classic novel, orphaned Fanny Hill is a prostitute who falls in love with a handsome merchant's son who also happens to be her first customer. 1✓

Fat Friends - 2000 to 2005 - This Yorkshire-based dramedy focuses on members of a weight loss group who become friends. 1__ 2__ 3__ 4__

Fingersmith - 2005 - In Victorian

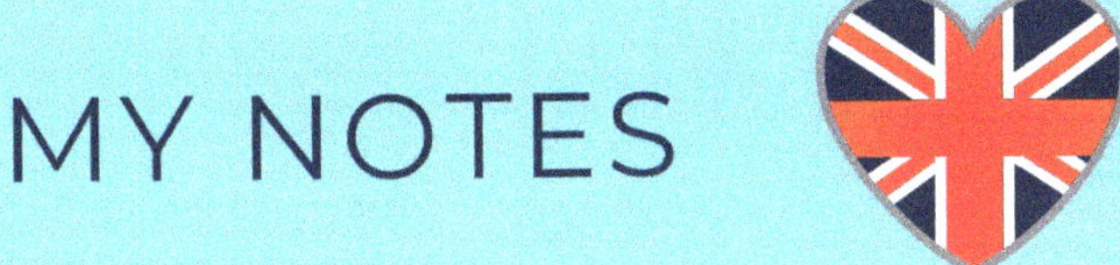
MY NOTES

England, a young woman becomes maid to a wealthy woman in order to carry out a criminal plot. M___

Firm Friends - 1992 to 1994 - A middle-class woman starts a catering business with her Indian housekeeper. 1___ 2___

Flambards - 1979 - When WWI arrives, orphaned Christina finds herself in charge of her uncle's estate. M___

Fleming - 2014 - This miniseries takes a look at the early life of James Bond creator Ian Fleming. M___

Follow Me - 1977 - A young boy longs for adventure, but he might have stumbled into more than he bargained for. 1___

Follyfoot - 1971 to 1973 - When a young woman is sent to stay in the country with her uncle, no one guesses it will quickly become the only place she feels happy. 1___ 2___ 3___

Forever Green - 1989 to 1992 - An inheritance allows a couple to abandon their lives in London and move to the countryside, but it's not without its issues. 1___ 2___

Fox - 1980 - This series about a South London gangland family was produced by Verity Lambert (*Doctor Who, Jonathan Creek*), and was ahead of its time in featuring the criminal as the protagonist. 1___

Frankie - 2013 - Eve Myles (*Keeping Faith*) stars as the head nurse on a traveling nursing team. 1___

From There to Here - 2014 - This family saga begins on the day of the 1996 Manchester bombing and continues on through 2000. 1___

Garrow's Law - 2009 to 2011 - This period legal drama was set in Georgian London and focused on the stories of real-life barrister William Garrow. 1___ 2___ 3___

Gazette - 1968 - A young Yorkshireman learns the newspaper business working at his father's paper, the Westdale Gazette. 1___

GBH - 1991 - This controversial period drama takes place toward the end of the Thatcher years, focusing on the intersection of an ambitious politician and well-liked headmaster of a local school. 1___

Gentleman Jack - 2018 to present - A woman comes back to her ancestral home, determined to restore it to its former glory. 1___

Gentlemen & Players - 1988 to 1989 - Two businessmen, one self-made and one not, constantly clash in a country village. 1___ 2___

Girlfriends - 2018 to present - A group of middle-aged women experience some strange and dramatic situations, but get through it together. 1✓

Goggle Eyes - 1993 - A young Honeysuckle Weeks (*Foyle's War*) stars in this series about a teen struggling to accept her divorced mother's attempts to date. M___

Gold Digger - 2019 - Julia Ormond stars in this miniseries about a woman entering into a relationship with a much younger man. M___

Goldplated - 2006 - A self-made

businessman attempts to close a big deal, but finds his shady past to be something of a hindrance. 1___

Goodnight Sweetheart - 1993 to 2016 - When a modern-day Londoner finds a portal back to World War II, he finds the era much more appealing than he might have guessed. 1___ 2___ 3___ 4___ 5___ 6___ 7___ | 2016 Reunion___

Gormenghast - 2000 - Christopher Lee and Jonathan Rhys Meyers star in this adaptation of Mervyn Peake's much-loved British fantasy series. M___

Great Expectations - 1981 - Joan Hickson plays Miss Havisham in this adaptation of the Dickens novel. M___

Great Expectations - 1989 - John Rhys-Davies and Anthony Hopkins appear in this British-American production of the Dickens novel. M___

Great Expectations - 2011 - This three-part adaptation of the Dickens novel by the same name is notable for featuring an exceptionally youthful Miss Havisham. M___

Guerilla - 2017 - This six-part miniseries focuses on the British black power movement of the early 1970s. M___

Gunpowder - 2017 - This miniseries focuses on the foiled 1605 Gunpowder Plot in London. M___

Gwaith/Cartref aka Work/Home - 2011 to present - This Welsh language drama follows a group of teachers working in a Welsh language school. 1___ 2___ 3___ 4___ 5___ 6___ 7___ 8___ 9___

Hadleigh - 1969 to 1976 - After inheriting a fortune, Hadleigh tires of leisure and opts for women and adventure. 1___ 2___ 3___ 4___

Hannay - 1988 to 1989 - Edwardian adventurer and outsider Richard Hannay is daring, clever, and good with the ladies. 1___ 2___

Hard Sun - 2018 to present - Though two detectives see things from vastly different perspectives, they're forced to work together to fight criminals in a world that may be doomed. 1___

Harlots - 2017 to present - While brothel owner Margaret Wells struggles to raise her daughters, a rival brothel owner targets her for attack. 1___ 2___

Harry - 1993 to 1995 - Harry Salter owns a news agency in Darlington, and he'll stop at nothing to get a story. 1___ 2___

Have Your Cake & Eat It - 1997 - A middle-aged roller coaster executive has an affair with a younger woman. M___

Headhunters - 1994 - James Fox and Francesca Annis star in this drama about a high-end headhunter who specializes in poaching the most talented executives. M___

Heartbeat - 1992 to 2009 - In this 1960s period drama, PC Nick Rowan is relocated to the tiny Yorkshire village where his wife grew up. 1___ 2___ 3___ 4___ 5___ 6___ 7___ 8___ 9___ 10___ 11___ 12___ 13___ 14___ 15___ 16___ 17___ 18___ | Changing Places Canadian Episode___ 10 Years of Heartbeat___ Heartbeat: Christmas Album___ Heartbeat: Farewell ***___ (Name omitted to avoid spoilers)

Hearts of Gold - 2003 - This two-part drama was based on Catrin Collier's first novel, and tells the story of a poor Welsh woman who falls in love with a well-to-do doctor. M___

Hetty Feather - 2015 to present - In this children's period drama set in Victorian London, a young orphan must return to the hospital where she was found. 1___ 2___ 3___ 4___

His Dark Materials - 2019 - Based on the Philip Pullman novel of the same name, this miniseries tells the story of two children adventuring through parallel universes. M___

Hold the Dream - 1987 - This follow-up to *A Woman of Substance* shows Emma Harte at 80. M___

Home Fires - 2015 to 2016 - This WWII-set series focused on the life of Women's Institute members in a rural Cheshire village. 1✓ 2✓

Hooten & the Lady - 2016 - A British Museum curator and American adventurer hunt treasures around the globe. 1___

Hope Springs - 2009 - Four English thieves hope to get out of the country, but instead end up in a small Scottish town. 1___

Hotel Babylon - 2006 to 2009 - Young and beautiful people work in a glamorous boutique hotel. 1___ 2___ 3___ 4___

How Green Was My Valley - 1976 – This miniseries adaptation of Richard Llewelyn's novel tells the story of the coal mining Morgan family in Wales. M___

Howards End - 2017 to 2018 - Based on the novel by E.M. Forster, this miniseries examines British class differences in early 1900s England by looking at three different families. M___

Howards' Way - 1985 to 1990 - When a man is made redundant from his job, he invests in an old boat yard. His family is not entirely supportive. 1___ 2___ 3___ 4___ 5___ 6___

Hustle - 2004 to 2012 - A group of con artists specializes in highly rewarding long cons. 1___ 2___ 3___ 4___ 5___ 6___ 7___ 8___

I, Claudius - 1976 - Derek Jacobi stars as Claudius in this history of the Roman Empire. M___

Ideal - 2005 to 2011 - Drug dealer Moz deals with the strange customers who come to his home to get high. 1___ 2___ 3___ 4___ 5___ 6___ 7___

In a Land of Plenty - 2001 - This period drama follows the industrialist Freeman family from 1952 on. 1___

In the Long Run - 2018 to present - In the 1980s, a black family in London sees their lives change dramatically when a relative from Africa comes to live with them. 1___ 2___

Injustice - 2011 - After a series of traumatic events shake his faith in the legal system, a barrister moves out to the countryside in hopes of peace and quiet. M___

Innocent - 2018 to present - When his conviction is overturned, David is released from a high security prison and begins to rebuild his life. 1___

Into the Labyrinth - 1981 to 1982 - When a group of children find a magician trapped the wall of a cave, they must help him regain his powers. 1___ 2___ 3___

Island at War - 2004 - During WW2, a quiet island community is disrupted by Nazi occupation. M___

Jack the Ripper - 1988 - Michael Caine stars as an inspector who starts off looking for Jack the Ripper and ends up uncovering a conspiracy. M___

Jamaica Inn - 2014 to 2015 - In 19th century Cornwall, a young woman living with her aunt and uncle discovers they are criminals. 1___

Jamestown - 2017 to present - Jamestown tells the story of English settlers in America during the early 1600s. 1___ 2___ 3___

Jane Eyre - 1983 - This 1983 adaptation of the classic novel features Timothy Dalton and Zelah Clarke. M___

Jane Eyre - 2007 - A young orphan becomes a governess and falls in love the with lord of the manor. M___

Jason King - 1972 - A former Department S intelligence agent travels the world writing trashy novels and taking on strange cases that frequently involve attractive women. 1___

Jennie: Lady Randolph Churchill - 1974 – This miniseries tells the story of American-born socialite and mother to Winston Churchill, Lady Randolph Churchill. M___

Jericho - 2016 - This Yorkshire-based 1870s period drama tells the story of a community dominated by the construction of a new viaduct. 1___

Jerusalem - 2019 to present - In 1940s Britain, a young woman's ambition leads her to become a spy for the Americans. 1___

Johnny Jarvis - 1983 - Two unlikely friends face adulthood and the end of school, each wondering whether their friendship can survive the transition. 1___

Jude the Obscure - 1971 - Born into poverty, a young man fights against his fate with little to show for it. M___

Justice - 2011 - This legal drama focuses on a small-town judge near Liverpool. M___

Karaoke - 1996 - When a girl from a karaoke bar is murdered, scriptwriter Daniel finds that real people seem to be speaking in the dialogue he's been writing. M___

King of the Castle - 1977 - This children's drama by Doctor Who writers Bob Baker and

Dave Martin follows a timid schoolboy who creates an elaborate pretend world and unintentionally finds himself transported into it. M___

Lady Chatterley - 1993 - Sean Bean and Judy Richardson star in this adaptation of the scandalous DH Lawrence novel. M___

Land Girls - 2009 to 2011 - Land Girls follows four women in the Women's Land Army during WW2. M___

Lark Rise to Candleford - 2008 to 2011 - In the 19th century, a girl moves to Oxfordshire to become a postmistress. 1___ 2___ 3___ 4___ | Christmas Special 2008___

Last Rights - 2005 - In a future 2009 London, voter apathy runs rampant and a new right-wing party comes into power with the goal of doing away with the democracy. M___

Last Tango in Halifax - 2012 to 2016 - Former childhood sweethearts, now in their 70s, reunite and fall in love. 1___ 2___ 3___ 4___

Les Misérables - 2018 - Adeel Akhtar and Olivia Colman star in this television adaptation of Victor Hugo's classic novel. M___

Life As I Know It - 2010 - This teen drama focuses on a group of young people starting out at The University of Manchester. 1___

Life Begins - 2004 to 2006 - When a thirtysomething couple goes on vacation with their teenagers, the father announces he wants a divorce to find himself. 1___ 2___ 3___

Life in Squares - 2015 - This miniseries focuses on The Bloomsbury Group, a group of early 20th century writers and intellectuals that included Virginia Woolf, E.M. Forster, and John Maynard Keynes. M___

Lilies - 2007 - After WWI, a widowed father raises his son and three daughters. M___

Lillie - 1978 - Beautiful Lillie Langtry attracts men and fame and trouble, remaining elegant and dignified all the while. M___

Little Dorrit – 2008 - With her father in debtor's prison, Amy Dorrit works hard to take care of the family. 1___

Little Napoleons - 1994 - This miniseries follows four politicians involved in local council elections. M___

Little Women - 2017 - With a cast that includes Angela Lansbury, this miniseries was adapted from the Louisa May Alcott book by the same name. M___

London's Burning - 1988 to 2002 - This series about a London fire brigade began as a TV movie and evolved into a long-running drama series. 1___ 2___ 3___ 4___ 5___ 6___ 7___ 8___ 9___ 10___ 11___ 12___ 13___ 14___ | 1986 TV Movie___ Christmas Special 1988___

Lorna Doone - 1976 to 1976 - This miniseries tells the story of star-crossed lovers in 17th century Somerset and Devon. M___

Lost in Austen - 2008 - A London-based Jane Austen fan is terribly surprised when she finds she's somehow swapped places with Elizabeth Bennet. M___

Love and Marriage - 2013 - Alison Steadman stars as a retired lollipop lady who decides to leave her family and live with her unconventional sister. 1___

Love for Lydia - 1977 - Edward wants heiress Lydia all to himself, but she craves excitement and prefers to flirt with many different men. 1___

Love Hurts - 1992 to 1994 - After a messy breakup, an ambitious woman leaves the rat race and finds herself pursued by a wealthy man who seems like trouble. 1___ 2___ 3___

Love in a Cold Climate - 2001 - Three privileged girls come of age between the wars. M___

Love in a Cold Climate - 1980 - Judi Dench stars in this miniseries about three privileged girls coming of age between the wars. M___

Love Life - 2012 - A man returns home from a trip abroad and discovers his ex-girlfriend is pregnant by her boss. 1___

Love, Lies, & Records - 2017 to present - Ashley Jensen (*Agatha Raisin*) stars as Kate Dickinson, a woman constantly challenged in her efforts to balance a personal life with the stress of the records she oversees. 1___

Love, Nina - 2016 - This miniseries offers a look at the 1980s literary scene in London. M___

Madame Bovary - 2000 - Based on the Flaubert novel, this miniseries tells the story of a woman who spends beyond her means to escape a boring life. M___

Maeve Binchy's Echoes - 1988 - In 1950s Ireland, a young woman longs to escape her tiny village, but local suitors may hamper her efforts. M___

Man at the Top - 1970 to 1972 - A Northern man tries to make his way in business down in the cutthroat southern part of the country. 1___ 2___

Man of the World - 1962 to 1963 - A journalist and his photographer travel the world, often finding themselves in the midst of glamour and intrigue. 1___ 2___

Mapp & Lucia - 1985 to 1986 - When Lucia moves to a small English village, she comes into conflict with Miss Mapp, a woman who controlled the social life in town before Lucia. 1___ 2___

Mapp & Lucia - 2014 - This three-part series was based on the Mapp & Lucia novels by E.F. Benson. M___

McMafia - 2018 to present - Alex, the English-born son of a Russian mafia member, attempts to live on the straight and narrow until a murder brings out his family history. 1___ 2___

Medici: Masters of Florence - 2016 to present - When Giovanni Medici is suddenly murdered, his sons must fight to keep the wealth and power of the family. 1___ 2___ 3___

Merlin - 1998 – Sam Neill and Helena Bonham Carter star in this miniseries adaptation of the Camelot story. M___

Merlin - 2008 to 2012 - A young sorcerer becomes best friends with Prince Arthur and they both become legends. 1___ 2___ 3___ 4___ 5___

Middlemarch - 1968 - Based on the George Eliot novel, the small town of Middlemarch faces the beginning of the Industrial Revolution. M___

Middlemarch - 1994 - Pam Ferris and Judi Dench both make appearances in this 1994 adaptation of the classic George Eliot novel. M✓

Mistresses - 2008 to 2010 - Mistresses focuses on the lives, loves, and affairs of four female friends. 1___ 2___ 3___

Monarch of the Glen - 2000 to 2005 - Young Archie MacDonald returns home to the Scottish Highlands to take his place as laird and save the family estate. 1___ 2___ 3___ 4___ 5___ 6___ 7___ | Hogmanay Special ___

Money - 2010 - John Self is good at making money, but he's better at spending it. M___

Monroe - 2011 to 2012 - James Nesbitt stars in this medical drama about a brilliant but quirky neurosurgeon and the talented doctors who work with him. 1___ 2___

Moondial - 1988 - A young girl finds a portal through time and discovers children who need her help. M___

MotherFatherSon - 2019 to present - Richard Gere stars alongside Billy Howle in this drama about an American businessman whose son runs his UK newspaper and starts down a self-destructive path. 1___

Moving On - 2009 to present - This anthology series of daytime plays always focuses on a person moving through a major life change of some sort. 1___ 2___ 3___ 4___ 5___ 6___ 7___ 8___ 9___

Mr. Wroe's Virgins - 1993 - Based on the novel by Jane Rogers, this series focuses on the seven young women who served a cult leader in 1830s Lancashire. M___

Mrs. Biggs - 2012 - This miniseries tells the story of Charmian Brent, a rebellious young woman whose relationship with the wrong man led to a descent into a crime. M___

Mrs. Wilson - 2019 - A woman is happily married to a mystery writer until he dies suddenly and another woman shows up claiming to be the real Mrs. Wilson. M___

My Brother Jonathan - 1985 - Daniel Day-Lewis stars in this miniseries about an idealistic doctor working in an area where poor industrial conditions cause numerous health issues. M___

My Mother & Other Strangers - 2016 to 2017 - A Northern Irish village struggles to maintain some semblance of normal life after a US military base is set up in the middle of town. 1___

My Uncle Silas - 2001 to 2003 - Based on stories by H.E. Bates, this series features a colorful Bedfordshire man. 1___ 2___

Nancherrow - 1999 - Joanna Lumley stars in this two-part miniseries about a colonel's daughter trying to maintain control of her family home. M___

Nancy Astor - 1982 - This miniseries

focuses on the first woman elected to the House of Commons. M___

National Treasure - 2016 - This drama about a comedian accused of raping a young girl was inspired by Operation Yewtree, a police operation that led to the prosecution of several celebrities. M___

New Worlds - 2014 - This sequel to *The Devil's Whore* focuses on changes on both sides of the pond in the 1680s. 1___

Newton's Law - 2017 to present - *Australia* - After her neighbourhood solicitor's office is burned down, a woman is persuaded to return to the high-flying world of Knox Chambers. 1___

Nicholas Nickelby - 1977 - A kind-hearted young man attempts to save his family from a cruel uncle. M___

Noah's Ark - 1997 to 1998 - In the Worcestershire countryside, an eccentric veterinarian treats animals with the help of his team. 1___ 2___

North & South - 1966 - In the fictional town of Milton, England, a transplanted Southern woman falls in love with a small-town Northerner. M___

Monarch of the Glen was filmed at Adverikie House in the Scottish Highlands. Today, fans can stay in self-catering cottages on the property and even hold weddings on-site.

North & South - 2004 - This miniseries is a modern update of the 60s adaptation of Elizabeth Gaskell's classic novel. M___

North Square - 2000 - This acclaimed but short-lived legal drama takes place at a defence chambers in Leeds. 1___

Notorious Woman - 1974 - Rosemary Harris (*Spiderman*) stars in this series about novelist George Sand and her romance with Frederic Chopin. M___

Number 10 - 1983 - This drama dives into the private lives on the men to occupy 10 Downing Street from the late 1700s to the early 1900s. 1___

Occupation - 2009 - Three British Army soldiers return to Morocco for different reasons - love, money, and personal convictions. 1___

Oliver Twist - 1985 - Miriam Margoyles and Lysette Anthony make appearances in this adaptation of the Dickens classic. M___

Oliver Twist - 1999 - Michael Kitchen, Julie Walters, and Keira Knightly all play roles in this version of the Dickens novel. M___

Oliver Twist - 2007 - Morven Christie, Tom Hardy, and Sarah Lancashire all appear in this star-studded adaptation of the Dickens classic. M___

One Child - 2016 - In this British-Chinese miniseries, a girl discovers she has a brother who's about to be put to death for a murder he didn't commit. M__

One Night - 2012 - In one night, four people are linked by an event in their area. M__

Onedin Line - 1971 to 1980 - In 1860s Liverpool, a man tirelessly attempts to establish a shipping line, marrying to get a ship and finding love. 1__ 2__ 3__ 4__ 5__ 6__ 7__ 8__

Ordinary Lies - 2015 to 2016 - Each series is set in a perfectly ordinary location, but the people have dark secrets. 1__ 2__

Orphan Black - 2013 to 2017 - *Canada* - When Sarah Manning witnesses the suicide of a woman who looks just like her, she begins down a path that leads to a much bigger conspiracy. 1__ 2__ 3__ 4__ 5__

Our Girl - 2013 to present - This military drama focuses on a working-class London girl who feels directionless and joins the military. 1__ 2__ 3__ 4__

Our Mutual Friend - 1998 - Based on the Dickens novel of the same name, this miniseries tells of love and greed in 1860s London. 1__

Our World War - 2014 - This miniseries attempts to tell the story of World War I through the eyes of soldiers. M__

Our Zoo - 2014 - This BBC One drama tells the story of George Mottershead and his journey to the creation of Chester Zoo. 1__

Out of the Unknown - 1965 to 1971 - This vintage anthology series features tales by science fiction greats like Frederik Pohl and Isaac Asimov. 1__ 2__ 3__ 4__

Outlander - 2014 to 2018 - In 1945, an English nurse is mysteriously transported back in time to Scotland in 1743. 1__ 2__ 3__ 4__ 5__ 6__

Overshadowed - 2017 - A young woman meets the personification of anorexia, and it becomes her destructive new best friend. M__

Oxbridge Blues - 1984 - This miniseries features seven unrelated teleplays about relationships. M__

Parade's End - 2013 - Benedict Cumberbatch stars in this series about a love triangle between an aristocrat, a socialite, and a suffragette. 1__

Paradox - 2009 - In this sci-fi police drama, a group of investigators look into evidence for events that haven't actually happened yet. 1__

Patrick Melrose - 2018 - Based on the semi-autobiographical Patrick Melrose novels by Edward St. Aubyn, this miniseries tells the story of an upper class man's addictions and family troubles. M__

Peaky Blinders - 2014 to present - Set in early 20th century Birmingham, this series focuses on gang boss Tommy Shelby and his family. 1__ 2__ 3__ 4__ 5__

Pen Talar - 2010 - This epic Welsh drama tells the story of two families over the course of half a century. 1__

Penmarric - 1979 - While his mother fights to gain control of Penmarric for her son

Mark, Mark has his own ideas about what he wants to do. 1___

Penny Dreadful - 2014 to 2016 - In Victorian England, an explorer, an American gunslinger, and a scientist fight dark forces. 1___ 2___ 3___

Performance - 1992 to 1998 - This anthology series focused on the production of classic and contemporary plays. 1___ 2___ 3___ 4___ 5___ 6___

Play for Today - 1970 to 1984 - This anthology series covered all genres and featured a number of acting standouts like Alison Steadman, Liz Smith, and Nigel Hawthorne. 1___ 2___ 3___ 4___ 5___ 6___ 7___ 8___ 9___ 10___ 11___ 12___ 13___ 1$___

Poldark - 2015 to 2019 - Aidan Turner stars in this remake of the story of Poldark, a man who returns home from the American Revolution to find both his fortunes and his love life in turmoil. 1___ 2___ 3___ 4___ 5___

Poldark - 1977 to 1978 - Ross Poldark returns home to Cornwall after the American Revolution, only to find his life in tatters. 1___ 2___

Portrait of a Marriage - 1990 - In Post-WWI England, two women embark on an illicit love affair that becomes increasingly destructive. M___

PREMature - 2015 - In West London, a young man comes of age and sees the people around him moving in two distinctly different directions. M___

Press - 2018 to present - This drama offers a glimpse into the private lives of hard-driving journalists under the pressure of the modern 24-hour news cycle. 1___

Pride & Prejudice - 1995 - Elizabeth Bennet tries her hand at love in Regency period England. M___

Prince Regent - 1979 - This miniseries tells the story of George, Prince of Wales, a man who waited almost 60 years for the throne. M___

Privates - 2013 - In 1960, eight young men are part of the last group of conscripts for National Service. 1___

Rain Shadow - 2007 - *Australia* - A veterinarian struggles to save a community ravaged first by drought, then by a sheep disease. M___

Rake - 2011 to 2018 - *Australia* - Defensc lawyer Cleaver Greene makes a career out of hopeless cases, perhaps because his own personal life is troubled enough to help him relate. 1___ 2___ 3___ 4___ 5___

Real Women - 1998 to 1999 - Five female friends reunite in London for a wedding and talk about the highs and lows of their lives. 1___ 2___

Reckless - 1997 - A young doctor returns home to Manchester to look after his sick father, then falls in love with his boss's wife. 1___ | Reckless: The Sequel Movie___

Red Letter Day - 1976 - This anthology series looks at red letter days for different characters. 1___

Red Rock - 2015 to present - *Ireland* - Members of the Red Rock Garda fight crime and protect citizens. 1__ 2__ 3__ 4__ 5__

Restless - 2012 - A young woman finds out her mother was a WW2 spy whose life hasn't been the same since. M__

Return of the Saint - 1978 to 1979 - Ian Ogilvy stars as Templar, a wealthy and mysterious do-gooder. 1__

Rocket Man - 2005 - A newly widowed man in Wales attempts to launch his wife's ashes into space. M__

Room at the Top - 2012 - This period drama is an adaptation of John Braine's novel about an ambitious young Yorkshireman in the 1940s. M__

Rosamunde Pilcher's Shades of Love - 2010 - This German production was set in Scotland and tells the story of a Scottish Laird with long-kept family secrets. 1__ 2__

Rumpole of the Bailey - 1978 to 1992 - Leo McKern starred as Horace Rumpole, a defense barrister who often took on underdog clients. 1__ 2__ 3__ 4__ 5__ 6__ 7__ | 1975 Play for Today Special__ 1980 Special __

Run - 2013 - This gritty four-part miniseries focuses on four people and the way their lives impact each other. M__

Sally Ann - 1979 - Stephanie Cole stars in this drama about a group of people involved with a Salvation Army center. 1__

Saracen - 1989 - David and Tom work for Saracen Systems, a private security firm with high-end clients and high-risk jobs. 1__

Screen One - 1989 to 1994 - This drama anthology series was created after Screen One, and designed for BBC1's more mainstream audience. 1__ 2__ 3__ 4__ 5__ 6__ | The Plant__ Trip Trap__ Killing Me Softly__ Truth or Dare__ Gobble__ Deacon Brodie__ Hostile Waters__ Our Boy__

Screen Two - 1985 to 1994 - This drama anthology series was originally created to air on BBC2. 1__ 2__ 3__ 4__ 5__

Screenplay - 1986 to 1993 - This series showcased feature-length television dramas. 1__ 2__ 3__ 4__ 5__ 6__ 7__ 8__

Seal Morning - 1986 - Based on the Rowena Farre novel, this serial tells the story of a child who goes to live with her aunt in a remote area, and the seal they raise together. 1__

Secret Diary of a Call Girl - 2007 to 2011 - Billie Piper (Doctor Who) stars as a high-end London call girl. 1__ 2__ 3__ 4__

Secret Smile - 2005 - When Miranda Cotton breaks up with her creepy boyfriend, he turns to her sister and is seen as the perfect son-in-law until strange things begin to happen to the family. M__

Secret State - 2012 - This political drama covers an investigation into safety procedures at a large petrochemical company after a devastating accident. M__

Secrets and Words - 2012 - This miniseries is a collection of dramatic episodes on the theme of adult literacy. M__

Sense & Sensibility - 2008 - When a woman finds herself newly widowed and

MY NOTES

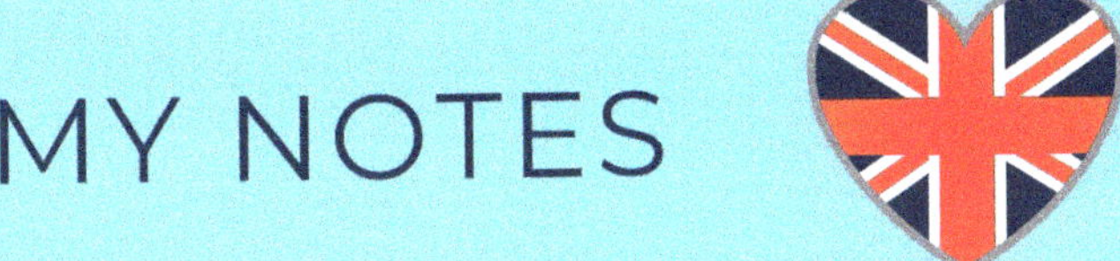

poor with three daughters, she downsizes and attempts to find good husbands for each of them. M__

Sharman - 1996 - Clive Owen stars in this crime drama series based on the Nick Sharman books by Mark Timlin. 1__

Shoebox Zoo - 2004 to 2005 - Alan Cumming and Rik Mayall star in this children's adventure series about a young American student studying in Edinburgh, whose toys come to life at night. 1__ 2__

Shoestring - 1979 to 1980 - Eddie Shoestring is a Talk radio detective. 1__ 2__

Silk - 2011 to 2014 - This legal drama focuses on London barristers from a set of criminal law chambers. 1__ 2__ 3__

Single Father - 2010 - David Tennant stars in this drama about a regular guy trying to raise his family after the death of his wife. M__

Six Face - 1972 - Six people meet a businessman, and he presents a different personality to each of them. 1__

Skins - 2007 to 2013 - This edgy drama is about a group of teens growing up in Bristol. 1__ 2__ 3__ 4__ 5__ 6__ 7__

Sky - 1975 - Three human teenagers help a lost young time traveler stranded on Earth. 1__

Smiley's People - 1982 - Based on a John Le Carre novel, British spymaster George Smiley is brought out of retirement by the murder of a Soviet defector he once handled. M__

Sons and Lovers - 1981 - This BBC adaptation of the DH Lawrence novel starred Eileen Atkins (*Cranford*). M__

Sorted - 2006 - This short-lived Manchester-based drama follows the personal and professional lives of a group of postmen. 1__

South Riding - 2011 - A left-wing Yorkshire headmistress feels deeply for the injustices faced by her students while also caring deeply for a Tory. M__

Sparkhouse - 2002 - This modern take on Wuthering Heights was written by screenwriter Sally Wainwright (*Happy Valley*). M__

Spies of Warsaw - 2013 - David Tennant stars in this drama about a military attaché at the French embassy in Warsaw when WW2 breaks out. M__

SS-GB - 2017 - This drama is set in an alternative timeline where the UK is occupied by the Nazis, and Winston Churchill has been executed. M__

Starlings - 2012 to 2013 - A working-class couple in Derbyshire brings grandpa into their crowded home. 1__ 2__

Steel River Blues - 2004 - This series examines the lives of a team of firefighters in Northeast England. 1__

Stella - 2012 to 2017 - A Welsh single mother holds her family together while struggling to make a living ironing. 1__ 2__ 3__ 4__ 5__ 6__ | Christmas Specials: 14__ 16__

Strangers & Brothers - 1984 - Anthony Hopkins portrays an ambitious lawyer in the years before WWII. 1___

Strike Back - 2010 to present - A secretive British military unit conducts covert intelligence operations around the globe. 1___ 2___ 3___ 4___ 5___ 6___

Striking Out - 2017 to 2018 - *Ireland* - After her husband and fellow solicitor cheats on her with a coworker, a woman quits to start her own firm. 1___ 2___

Summer of Rockets - 2019 - This Cold War-era drama focuses on a Russian-Jewish inventor and his family as they live in an increasingly tense Britain. M___

Sword of Honour - 1986 - This miniseries takes a look at some of Britain's military heroes and the price they paid, both at home and abroad. M___

Taboo - 2017 to present - An adventurer returns home to London to rebuild the family business during the War of 1812. 1___ 2___

Take Me - 2001 - Robson Green stars in this drama about a couple that moves into a new home, only to find themselves in a strange web of illicit secrets with their neighbours. M___

Tales from Pleasure Beach - 2001 - This miniseries presents three different tales that all happen at the same Welsh resort. M___

Tales of the City - 1994 - This British-American miniseries is based on Armistead Maupin's book about colorful people living in San Francisco. M___

Tales of Uplift and Moral Improvement - 2001 - Each week, an Edwardian narrator (Rik Mayall) presents period dramas about children in morally challenging circumstances. 1___

Teachers - 2001 to 2004 - Andrew Lincoln (*The Walking Dead*) stars in this early 2000s series about the exploits of teachers both in and out of the classroom. 1___ 2___ 3___ 4___

Temple - 2019 to present - This series is a remake of the Norwegian medical drama *Valkyrien*, about a surgeon who is pushed to the limit in his attempts to save his dying wife. 1___

Tenko - 1981 to 1984 - In 1942, a group of British, Australian, and Dutch women are held in a Japanese internment camp. 1___ 2___ 3___

Tess of the D'Urbervilles - 2009 - In this miniseries based on the Thomas Hardy work, Tess Durbeyfield is a poor country girl with connections to nobility. M___

The 7.39 - 2014 - When they meet while fighting for a seat on the morning commute, a young couple can't help falling in love. M___

The A Word - 2016 to present - When their son is diagnosed with autism, a family struggles to come to terms with what that means for them. 1___ 2___

The Adventurer - 1972 to 1974 - Wealthy Gene Bradley is a government agent who poses as an actor. 1___

The Afternoon Play - 2003 to 2007 - This dramatic anthology features a different contemporary drama in each episode. 1___

2___ 3___ 4___ 5___

The Ambassador - 1998 to 1999 - Harriet wants to move on from her husband's murder when she becomes the British Ambassador to Ireland. Her son refuses to accept her new role. 1___ 2___

The Assets - 2014 - While this series about real life traitor and double agent Aldrich Ames is American, it's almost entirely cast with British actors. M___

The Barchester Chronicles - 1982 - A small village gets riled up when the local church becomes embroiled in scandal. M___

The Beggar Bride - 1997 - A young married woman begins an affair with an older man in an attempt to get money. 1___

The Blue Rose - 2013 - *New Zealand* - Support workers at a big city law firm band together to get justice for an employee with a highly suspicious death. 1___

The Bretts - 1987 to 1989 - This period drama features a family of actors making their way in the 1920s. 1___ 2___

The Broker's Man - 1997 to 1998 - An ex-policeman uses his investigative skills to help insurance companies fight frauds. 1___ 2___

The Brontes of Haworth - 1973 - In West Yorkshire, three of England's greatest writers come of age. M___

The Brothers - 1972 to 1976 - When a man dies while making love to his secretary, his sons take over the family trucking business. 1___ 2___ 3___ 4___ 5___ 6___ 7___

The Buddha of Suburbia - 1993 - A young man with an English mother and Indian father struggles to find his place in an often-racist society. 1___

The Camomile Lawn - 1992 - In 1939, five cousins gather at a family home on the Cornish Coast to enjoy one last hurrah before the onset of WW2. They reunite 50 years later to look back on how the war shaped their lives. M___

The Casual Vacancy - 2015 - When a councilman unexpectedly dies, the vacancy on the council becomes a battleground for the small town's secrets. M___

The Cazalets - 2001 - This six-part series tells the story of The Cazalet family during WW2. M___

The Cedar Tree - 1976 to 1978 - An

aristocratic British family makes its way through the 1930s. 1___ 2___ 3___ 4___

The Changes - 1975 - This progressive sci-fi series features a particularly unsettling depiction of society in meltdown. M___

The Clinic - 2003 to 2009 - *Ireland* - This drama focuses on a group of medical professionals in a busy Dublin clinic. 1___ 2___ 3___ 4___ 5___ 6___ 7___ 8___ 9___

The Code - 2014 to 2016 - *Australia* - Two Australian hackers find themselves caught up in matters of national security and large-scale corruption. 1___ 2___

The Collection - 2016 - In Post-WW2 Paris, drama unfolds in a family fashion business. 1 ___

The Commander - 2003 to 2008 - This series of television movies focuses on a female commander in the male-dominated Metropolitan Police Service. 1___ 2___ 3___ 4___ 5___

The Crimson Field - 2014 to 2015 - At a busy WWI hospital, Kitty tries to escape her past. 1___

The Crimson Petal & the White - 2011 - In 1870s London, a woman gains power by becoming the mistress of a powerful man. M___

The Crown - 2016 to 2019 - This historical drama chronicles the reign of Queen Elizabeth II, beginning with her marriage to Philip, Duke of Edinburgh. 1___ 2___ 3___

The Darling Buds of May - 1991 to 1993 - A young Catherine Zeta-Jones appears in this series about a farming family in Kent. 1___ 2___ 3___

The Deep - 2010- James Nesbitt and Minnie Driver star in this drama about disaster on a research submarine. 1___

The Devil's Whore - 2008 - This miniseries tells the story of the English Civil War through the eyes of a teenage girl. M___

The Diary of Anne Frank - 2009 - This BBC production tells the story of Anne Frank as she hid from the Nazis in Amsterdam. M___

The District Nurse - 1984 to 1987 - This period drama follows the true-life story of a Welsh nurse working hard to improve conditions for residents of a small mining town. 1___ 2___ 3___

The Duchess of Duke Street - 1976 to 1977 - In Victorian London, a young woman learns to cook under a pompous French chef. 1___

The Dumping Ground - 2013 to present – Though it's set in a children's home referred to as the "dumping ground", the kids who live there still have fun. 1___ 2___ 3___ 4___ 5___ 6___

The Durrells aka The Durrells in Corfu - 2016 to present - When a woman's life falls apart, she decides to take her children and get a fresh start on a Greek island. 1___ 2___ 3___ 4___

The Escape Artist - 2013 - David Tennant stars as a promising barrister who excels at getting his clients out of bad situations. M___

The Far Pavilions - 1984 - This epic tale of forbidden love in colonial India is set against their revolution for freedom from England. M___

The First - 2018 to present - This British-American co-production features a group of astronauts as they become the first to visit Mars. 1___

The Flame Trees of Thika - 1981 - Hayley Mills stars in this WWI-era period drama about a young woman whose parents decide to start a coffee plantation in Africa. M___

The Flaxton Boys - 1969 to 1973 - This children's adventure drama traces the lives of several generations of the Yorkshire-based Flaxton family. 1___ 2___ 3___ 4___

The Flower of Gloster - 1967 - This children's show stars a canal barge that winds its way around England and Wales, mixing adventure and history. 1___

The Fragile Heart - 1996 - While traveling in China, a cardiac surgeon finds himself faced with an ethical dilemma over human rights. 1___

The Game - 2014 - Set in 1970s London, this spy thriller follows Tom Hughes as a troubled young MI-5 operative. 1___

The Glittering Prizes - 1976 - This miniseries follows the lives of Cambridge undergrads over 20 years as they learn about real life. M___

The Good Karma Hospital - 2017 to present - Broken-hearted Doctor Ruby Walker goes to India to lose herself in the job, but she doesn't expect the life she finds. 1___ 2___ 3___

The Governor - 1995 to 1996 - Helen Hewitt is the first woman to oversee Barfield, a maximum security prison riddled with problems. 1___ 2___

The Great Fire - 2014 - This four-part miniseries is set during the Great Fire of London in 1666, focusing on the family whose bakery was the origin of the fire. M___

The Halcyon - 2017 - A glamorous five-star hotel in 1940s London plays host to all kinds of drama. 1___

The Heart Guy aka Doctor Doctor - 2016 to present - *Australia* - After some troubles, a rising heart surgeon is reassigned as a country doctor. 1___ 2___ 3___ 4___

The History Man - 1981 - A liberal history professor subtly controls many of his students and his colleagues. 1___

The Hollow Crown - 2013 to 2016 - This miniseries features short adaptations of Shakespearean plays. M___

The House of Eliott - 1991 to 1994 - When their father dies and leaves them in debt, two sisters struggle to start a dressmaking business. 1___ 2___ 3___

The Indian Doctor - 2010 to 2013 - An Indian doctor moves to a small Welsh mining village during the 1960s. 1___ 2___ 3___

The Irish R.M. - 1983 to 1985 - *Ireland* - When an Englishman leaves home to become an Irish Resident Magistrate, he quickly learns the normal rules don't apply with his eccentric new neighbours. 1___ 2___ 3___

The Jensen Code - 1973 - In this children's thriller, a young boy disappears for hours and has no recollection of his absence. 1___

The Kids from 47A - 1973 to 1974 - With their Dad away from home and their mother in the hospital, a group of kids struggle to hide the fact that they've no parents at home. 1___ 2___ 3___

The Lakes - 1997 to 1999 - John Simm (*Life on Mars*) stars as a hotel porter, gambler, and philanderer living in the Lake District. 1___ 2___

The Last Kingdom - 2015 to 2018 - As the Danes conquer one English kingdom after another, all that remains is Wessex. 1___ 2___ 3___

The Last Post - 2017 - This miniseries tells the story of the women and children alongside British Army soldiers fighting a 1965 Yemeni insurgency. M___

The Life & Times of David Lloyd George - 1981 - This short series offers a look at the life of David Lloyd George, the last Liberal Prime Minister of the UK. M___

The Little Drummer Girl - 2018 - Set in 1979, this series shows an idealistic young woman who is quickly drawn into a complex international spy plot. M___

The Little House - 2010 - As a young mother struggles to bond with her baby, her manipulative mother-in-law tries to gain control of the child. 1___

The Lotus Eaters - 1972 to 1973 - A couple runs a bar on a Greek island, and each have shady pasts. 1___ 2___

The Main Chance - 1969 to 1975 - After starting out in London, a compassionate but ambitious young lawyer returns home to Leeds to establish his own practice. 1___ 2___ 3___ 4___

The Master of Ballantrae - 1975 - Based on the Robert Lewis Stevenson novel, brothers toss a coin to see who joins Prince Charlie during the Jacobite rising, and who stays behind to oversee the family home. M___

The Mill - 2013 to 2014 – This series focuses on the challenging, often abusive conditions endured by cotton mill workers. 1___ 2___

The Mill on the Floss - 1978 to 1979 - In early 1800s England, Maggie creates a rift between herself and her brother when she stands by the man she loves. M___

The Miniaturist - 2017 - When a young woman in 17th century Amsterdam hires a miniaturist to furnish her dollhouse, she's surprised to see the miniatures providing clues to her future. M___

The Musketeers - 2014 to 2016 - This adaptation of the Dumas novel includes Tom Burke, Peter Capaldi, and Rupert Everett. 1___ 2___ 3___

The Nativity - 2010 - This retelling of the birth of Jesus features Tatiana Maslany, Neil Dudgeon, Andrew Buchan, and Peter Capaldi. M___

The Old Curiosity Shop - 1979 to 1980 -

Nell lives and works with her grandfather in a London shop until they are forced out because of her grandfather's gambling debts. M___

The Onedin Line - 1971 to 1980 - Set in 1880 Liverpool, James marries in order to get a ship and start his own shipping line. 1___ 2___ 3___ 4___ 5___ 6___ 7___ 8___

The Organization - 1972 - This drama focuses on the lives of executives at a faceless corporation called The Greatrick Organization. 1___

The Outcast - 2015 - After witnessing the death of his mother, a grief-stricken young boy is sent to live with a father he barely knows. M___

The Owl Service - 1969 to 1970 - While on holiday in a remote Welsh valley, a young girl and her step-brother unintentionally bring an ancient legend back to life. 1___

The Palace - 2008 - After the death of King James III, his unsuitable son ascends the throne and nearly tears the monarchy to bits. 1___

The Pallisers - 1974 to 1975 - Set against the backdrop of the House of Commons, this miniseries looks at the lives of Glencora's family after her forced marriage. M___

The Paper Lads - 1977 to 1979 – This Newcastle-based children's series focuses on kids who deliver newspapers. 1___ 2___

The Paradise - 2012 to 2013 - In this period drama, a young and ambitious woman heads to the city to make her way working in a department store. 1___ 2___

The Passing Bells - 2014 - This British-Polish drama tells the story of two teens, one British and one German, who sign up to fight in WWI. M___

The Phoenix and the Carpet - 1976 to 1977 - Children discover an egg that hatches into a magical phoenix. M___

The Pickwick Papers - 1985 - This twelve-part adaptation of Dickens's *The Pickwick Papers* includes familiar faces like Nigel Stock and Patrick Malahide. M___

The Politician's Husband - 2013 - David Tennant and Emily Watson star in this drama about a wife whose career begins to outshine that of her husband. M___

The Politician's Wife - 1995 - A woman finds out that her husband, a member of Parliament, has been having an affair with a prostitute. M___

The Portrait of a Lady - 1968 - A young American woman enters into a terrible marriage in 1800s Italy. M___

The Power Game - 1965 to 1969 - John Wilder doesn't let anything get in the way of his large and growing business. 1___ 2___ 3___

The Price - 1985 - A wealthy Irish businessman's wife is kidnapped by the IRA. M___

The Promise - 2011 - A young British girl travels to Israel to retrace her grandfather's military service. M___

The Railway Children - 1968 - Jenny Agutter (*Call the Midwife*) stars in this adaptation of the much-loved Edith Nesbit serial. M___

The Rector's Wife - 1994 - A rector's wife feels underappreciated, gets a job, and has an affair. M___

The Refugees - 2014 to 2015 - *Spain* - Refugees from the future travel to the present to escape global disaster in this Spanish-British co-production. M___

The Royal - 2003 to 2011 - This medical drama began as a spinoff to *Heartbeat*, set in a hospital often used to treat the characters in *Heartbeat*. 1___ 2___ 3___ 4___ 5___ 6___ 7___ 8___

The Saint - 1962 to 1969 - Roger Moore stars as "The Saint", a wealthy adventurer who travels around stealing from the rich and giving to the poor. 1___ 2___ 3___ 4___ 5___ 6___

The Saint - 1989 to 1990 - Simon Dutton (*Doctors*) starred as Simon Templar in this series of television movies based on the Leslie Charteris novels: The Brazilian Connection, The Blue Dulac, Wrong Number, Fear in Fun Park, and The Big Bang. M___

The Paradise was filmed in County Durham at Lambton Castle, which was converted to look like an 1800s department store. Other shops were built for the production. Today, it serves as a wedding and event venue.

The Sentimental Agent - 1963 - This spinoff of *Man of the World* sees Carlos Varelas in London, solving problems and rescuing damsels in distress. 1___

The Siege of Golden Hill - 1975 to 1976 - When an old man is threatened with eviction from his home, there's no one to help him except his gang member grandson. 1___ 2___

The Silver Chair - 1990 - This British-American family adventure series sees Eustace returning to Narnia with a new companion. M___

The Slap - 2011 - When someone slaps a child who isn't his own, the repercussions echo through an entire group of friends. M___

The Smoke - 2014 - This drama focuses on a team of talented London firefighters and includes Jodie Whittaker (*Doctor Who*). 1___

The Split - 2018 to 2019 - When their father returns after having been out of their lives for 30 years, a family of female lawyers must confront their shared past. 1___

The State - 2017 - *The State* follows four British citizens who leave Britain to join ISIS. 1___

The State Within - 2006 - This miniseries follows the British Ambassador to America during an imminent threat to Western democracy. M___

The Story of Tracy Beaker - 2002 to 2006 - A ten-year-old girl who lives in a children's home makes mischief and friends wherever she goes. 1___ 2___ 3___ 4___ 5___

The Street - 2006 to 2008 - Each episode takes a look at what's going on with a different family who lives on the same street. 1___ 2___ 3___

The Syndicate - 2012 to 2015 - In each series, a different syndicate of coworkers wins the lottery, with dramatic consequences. 1___ 2___ 3___

The Tenant of Wildfell Hall - 1996 - A young woman and her son move to Yorkshire, but keep to themselves until a charming farmer comes along. 1___

The Troubleshooters aka Mogul - 1965 to 1972 - This business drama focuses on an oil company and its chief troubleshooter. 1___ 2___ 3___ 4___ 5___ 6___ 7___

The Tudors - 2007 to 2010 - *The Tudors* is a drama about Henry VIII and his extensive love life. 1___ 2___ 3___ 4___

In 2013, The Syndicate was adapted into an American series called Lucky 7. It failed terribly, and only two episodes were ever broadcast - though all eight episodes are available for purchase.

The Village - 2013 to 2014 - This drama tells the story of life in a Derbyshire village from the perspective of villager Bert Middleton. 1___ 2___

The Virtues - 2019 to present - *Ireland* - A troubled man returns to Ireland to confront his unhappy past in the child care system. 1___

The Way We Live Now - 2001 - Based on the novel by Anthony Trollope, this miniseries covers the life of mysterious financier Augustus Melmotte. M___

The White Princess - 2017 - The White Princess is a sequel to The White Queen, an adaptation of Philippa Gregory's historic novel. M___

The White Queen - 2013 - Three relentless and manipulative women seek the crown in 15th century England. M___

The Widow - 2018 to present - Kate Beckinsale stars in this series about a woman who sees the husband she believes to be dead on the news. 1___

The Woman in White - 1982 - In Victorian England, a mysterious doppelganger, the woman in white, may hold the key to a frightening mystery. M___

The Woman in White - 2018 - Jessie Buckley stars in this adaptation of the Wilkie Collins gothic novel. M___

The Zoo Gang - 1974 - Four people who worked together on cases during the war had code names based on animals, so they called them the Zoo Club. They still work together occasionally. 1___

There She Goes - 2018 to present - David

Tennant stars in this family comedy-drama about a young girl with severe learning disabilities. 1___

Therese Raquin - 1980 - This tale of passion and obsession is based on the novel by Emile Zola. M___

This is England 86 - 2010 - This spinoff of the 2006 film *This is England* focuses on members of the mod revival scene. M___

This is England 88 - 2011 - This sequel to *This is England 86* focuses on the same cast of characters, 2 years later. M___

This is England 90 - 2015 - Friends from the previous *This is England* installments are reunited in the midst of 1990s rave culture. M___

Thomas & Sarah - 1979 - This spinoff of *Upstairs Downstairs* follows two characters from the earlier series. M___

Three Girls - 2017 - Authorities ignore the trafficking of young girls by British Pakistani men. 1___

Tina & Bobby - 2017 - This miniseries follows the relationship of Tina Dean and her West Ham United footballer husband, Bobby Moore. M___

Tinsel Town - 2000 to 2001 - Dawn Steele (*Monarch of the Glen*) appears in this BBC drama that takes place in the Glasgow club scene. 1___ 2___

Tipping the Velvet - 2002 - This period drama tells the story of a love affair between two music hall women in the 1890s. 1___

Titanic - 2012 - This retelling of the Titanic's sinking was written by Julian Fellowes (*Downton Abbey*) to mark the 100th anniversary of the disaster. M___

tlc - 2002 - A new doctor finds himself in a bit over his head when he starts working in the darkly surreal South Middlesex Hospital. 1___

To Serve Them All My Days - 1980 to 1981 - Injured and shell-shocked from WWI, David takes a job in a boy's school. 1___

Traffik - 1989 - Vastly different people from all walks of life intersect in an international story about heroin and drug trafficking. 1___

Trauma - 2018 to present - This thriller shows how two fathers' lives collide when one man's son dies at the hands of the other. 1___

Triangle - 1981 to 1983 - A ferry crew in the North Sea runs a triangular route between Amsterdam, Felixstowe, and Gothenburg. 1___ 2___ 3___

Troy: Fall of a City - 2018 - This miniseries is a retelling of the siege of Troy, loosely based on the Iliad. M___

Truckers - 2013 - This drama revolves around the lives of truck drivers in Nottingham. 1___

True Love aka Love Life - 2012 - This series tells five tales of different people dealing with love and life. M___

Trust - 2003 - Robson Green and Sarah Parish star in this often-humorous legal drama about a brash lawyer who uses unconventional logic to win his cases. 1___

Trust - 2018 - This British-American

production tells the story of the Getty family and the 1973 kidnapping and ransom of John Paul Getty III. 1___

Tutankhamun - 2016 - This adventure miniseries is based on Howard Carter's discovery of King Tut's tomb. M___

Tutti Frutti - 1987 - Robbie Coltrane stars as an aging Scottish rock and roll star. 1___

Twenty Thousand Streets Under the Sky - 2005 - This miniseries focuses on the lives and loves of working-class Londoners in the 1930s. M___

Two Thousand Acres of Sky - 2001 to 2003 - A single mother with two children moves from the inner city to a small Scottish village to improve their lives. 1___ 2___ 3___

Under the Mountain - 1983 - *New Zealand* - While on vacation in Auckland, two teens meet a man who turns out to be an alien in need of assistance. 1___

Upstairs Downstairs - 1971 to 1977 - This drama follows the aristocratic Bellamy family and the servants who live downstairs. 1___ 2___ 3___ 4___ 5___ | 1996 Anniversary Show___

Upstairs Downstairs - 2010 to 2012 - This drama reveals the lives of a well-off family upstairs and their servants who live downstairs. 1___ 2___

Vanity Fair - 2018 - Becky Sharp climbs out of poverty and into English society, climbing all the way to King George IV's court. M___

Versailles - 2015 to present - King Louis XIV of France plans to create the greatest palace in the world. 1___ 2___ 3___

Victoria - 2016 to present - Victoria comes to the British throne at 18 and marries Prince Albert. 1___ 2___ 3___

Wanderlust - 2018 to present - Toni Collette and Steven Mackintosh star as a mid-life couple in a sexual rut. 1___

War & Peace - 2007 - This 2007 adaptation of Tolstoy's classic includes an appearance by Brenda Blethyn (*Vera*). M___

War & Peace - 2016 - This miniseries adaptation tells the story of five aristocratic families in Russia whose lives will be changed by the Napoleonic conflict. M___

We'll Meet Again - 1982 - In a small English town during WWII, American Air Force men don't always get along with the locals. 1___

Wessex Tales - 1973 - The short tales of Thomas Hardy are told in this series. M___

When the Boat Comes In - 1976 to 1981 - In between the wars, an ex-sergeant returns home to his poverty-stricken village in northeastern England. 1___ 2___ 3___ 4___

Where the Heart Is - 1997 to 2006 - This long-running drama follows a group of nurses in a small Yorkshire town. 1___ 2___ 3___ 4___ 5___ 6___ 7___ 8___ 9___ 10___

White Heat - 2012 - This miniseries follows seven London students as they age, with each episode taking place in a different year. M___

Who Pays the Ferryman? - 1977 – A man attempts to track down an old love and finds out she's passed away, leaving behind a daughter he never knew about. 1___

Wild at Heart - 2006 to 2013 - A veterinarian travels to South Africa with his family to release a wild animal at a game reserve, but then decides to stay and manage the reserve. 1___ 2___ 3___ 4___ 5___ 6___ 7___ 8___

Wives & Daughters – 1971 - In this period drama, Molly and her widower father live alone happily until he remarries and throws her life into turmoil. M___

Wives and Daughters - 1999 - In this reboot of the 1971 miniseries, Molly and her widower father live alone happily until he remarries and throws her life into turmoil. M___

Wolf Hall - 2015 - This period miniseries follows the events after the downfall of Cardinal Wolsey when his secretary, Thomas Cromwell, gets close to the king. M___

Women in Love - 2011 - This two-part miniseries is based on two DH Lawrence novels, *The Rainbow* and *Women in Love*. M___

World Without End - 2012 - The English town of Kingsbridge deals with the start of the Hundred Years' War and looming threat of the Black Death. M___

Wreckers at Dead Eye - 1970 - On a dark and stormy night in 1770, a ship crashes, led astray by the light of a smuggling operation along the coast. M___

Wuthering Heights - 2009 - The dark and destructive love between Catherine and Healthcliff threatens the peaceful existence of everyone around them. M___

Years and Years - 2019 to present - This series focuses on a Manchester family, beginning in 2019 before flashing fifteen years ahead to a very different England. 1___

Young James Herriot - 2011 - This miniseries focuses on the early life of famed veterinarian James Herriot. M___

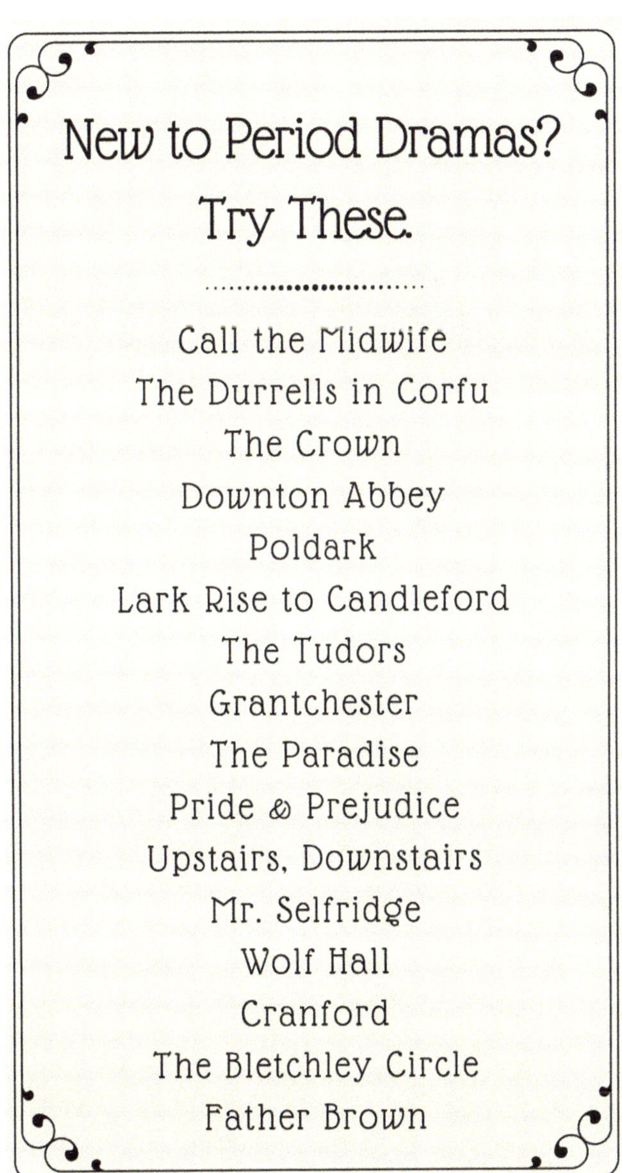

Castles - 1995 to 1995 - This short-lived soap opera followed three generations of the London-based Castle family, and included a young Sally Wainwright (*Happy Valley*) on its writing staff. 1__ 2__ 3__ 4__ 5__ 6__ 7__ 8__ 9__ 10__ 11__ 12__ 13__ 14__ 15__ 16__ 17__ 18__ 19__ 20__ 21__ 22__ 23__ 24__

Casualty - 1986 to 2018 - This series is all about the lives of the people in the emergency department at Holby City Hospital. 1__ 2__ 3__ 4__ 5__ 6__ 7__ 8__ 9__ 10__ 11__ 12__ 13__ 14__ 15__ 16__ 17__ 18__ 19__ 20__ 21__ 22__ 23__ 24__ 25__ 26__ 27__ 28__ 29__ 30__ 31__ 32__ 33__

Coronation Street - 1960 to 2018 - This iconic British soap follows a community of working-class people in Manchester. 9698 episodes

Crossroads - 1964 to 1988 and 2001 to 2003 - This low-budget soap opera centered around a fictional motel in the Midlands. First Run: 4510 episodes Revival: 320 episodes

Doctors - 2000 to 2018 - This Midlands-based soap follows the lives of medical staff at two medical facilities. 1__ 2__ 3__ 4__ 5__ 6__ 7__ 8__ 9__ 10__ 11__ 12__ 13__ 14__ 15__ 16__ 17__ 18__ 19__

Eastenders - 1985 to 2018 - This classic British soap deals with the working-class people around Albert's Square in the East End of London. 5809 episodes

Eldorado - 1992 to 1993 - Verity Lambert (*Doctor Who*) executive-produced this series about mostly British ex-pats in Spain. 156 episodes

Garnock Way - 1976 to 1979 - This Scottish drama was set in a fictional mining town between Glasgow and Edinburgh, and was deemed too gritty to be shown on some channels. 173 episodes

Holby City - 1999 to 2018 - This series follows the lives of staff, patients and others at Holby City General Hospital. 1__ 2__ 3__ 4__ 5__ 6__ 7__ 8__ 9__ 10__ 11__ 12__ 13__ 14__ 15__ 16__ 17__ 18__ 19__ 20__

Hollyoaks - 1995 to 2018 - Set in a fictional suburb of Chester, this series follows a group of mostly young characters as they deal with life and love. 1__

Hollyoaks Later - 2008 to 2013 - *Hollyoaks Later* was designed as a late-night spinoff to *Hollyoaks* to allow them to explore darker and more sexual content. 1___ 2___ 3___ 4___ 5___ 6___

London Bridge - 1996 to 1999 - This series focused on a group of young adults living in a converted mill in London. 1___ 2___ 3___ 4___

Machair - 1993 to 1998 - This Scottish drama was set on the Isle of Lewis in the Outer Hebrides and broadcast in Gaelic with English subtitles. 1___ 2___ 3___ 4___ 5___ 6___ 7___ 8___ 9___ 10___ 11___ 12___

Night & Day - 2001 to 2003 - This early 2000s soap is set in Greenwich and centers around a group of friends as they raise their families. 1___ 2___ 3___

Quayside - 1997 to 1997 - This short-lived soap opera covered the lives of a group of young people living on the Newcastle Quayside. 1___

Revelations - 1994 to 1996 - This late-night soap is a drama about the family of an Anglican priest and his wife. 1___ 2___

River City - 2002 to present - This Scottish soap opera focuses on the lives of a group of people in Glasgow. 1___ 2___ 3___ 4___ 5___ 6___ 7___ 8___ 9___ 10___ 11___ 12___ 13___ 14___ 15___ 16___ 17___ 18___ 19___ 20___

Take the High Road - 1980 to 2003 - This soap opera focuses on the residents of Glendarroch, a small Scottish Village. 1___ 2___ 3___ 4___ 5___ 6___ 7___ 8___ 9___

The Cut - 2009 to 2010 - This youth-oriented soap was broadcast in 5-minute daily increments online over the course of two years. 1___ 2___ 3___

A Great Welsh Adventure with Gryff Rhys Jones - 2014 - Griff takes us on a beautiful journey through his native Wales. M__

Alistaire Cooke's America - 1972 - Anglo-American journalist Alistaire Cooke covers the history of the US up until the early 1970s. M__

Ancient Invisible Cities - 2018 - Michael Scott teams up with subject-matter experts in different locales to reveal hidden secrets beneath the world's oldest cities. M__

Around the World in 80 Gardens - 2008 - Monty Don visits some of the most unique gardens in the world M__

Back in Time for Tea - 2018 - This series looks at how Northern English cuisine has changed over the past 100 years. M__

Barging Round Britain with John Sergeant - 2015 to 2016 - Former journalist John Sergeant takes viewers all over Britain, from the Hebrides Islands of Scotland to the county of Somerset. 1__ 2__

Baroque! From St. Peter's to St. Paul's - 2009 - This three-part BBC Four documentary focuses on art and architecture from the Baroque period. M__

Best Walks with a View - 2016 to present - Walking enthusiast Julia Bradbury takes viewers on some her favorite highly-accessible treks around Britain. 1__ 2__

Bill Bryson Notes from a Small Island - 1999 - Bill Bryson takes viewers on a trip around Great Britain. M__

Birding with Bill Oddie - 1997 to 2000 - This loosely-scripted documentary follows writer and conservationist Bill Oddie as he observes birds in their natural habitat. 1__ 2__ 3__

Bloody Britain - 2004 - Comedian Rory McGrath looks into the gruesome past of Britain. M__

Britain's Great Cathedrals with Tony Robinson - 2018 - Tony Robinson visits some of Britain's most awe-inspiring cathedrals, focusing on their history and how they've shaped their communities. M__

Britain's Lost Routes - 2012 - Griff Rhys Jones looks at ancient routes associated with the movement of different people or products in Britain. M__

Britain's Most Historic Towns - 2018 to present - Professor Alice Roberts gives viewers history lessons as she travels around Britain. 1__

British Gardens in Time - 2014 - Paul Copley (*Downton Abbey*) narrates this series that visits four exquisite gardens in the UK. M__

Cathedral Cities - 2012 - This six-part series explores what makes English cathedral cities so special, and includes visits to cities like Portsmouth, Rochester, Salisbury, and more. M__

Charlie Luxton's Homes by the Sea - 2014 to 2015 - Architect Charlie Luxton travels around Britain checking out unique homes along the coastline. 1__ 2__

Churches: How to Read Them - 2010 - Dr. Richard Taylor examines the imagery, symbols, and architecture of Britain's churches. M__

Churchill's Bodyguard - 2005 - This 13-part series is based on the memoir of Walter Thompson, Churchill's long-time personal bodyguard. M__

Civilisation - 1969 to 1970 - This ambitious documentary series by Kenneth Clarke looks at the history and cultural heritage of the western world. M__

Civilisations - 2018 - With nearly 50 years passing since Kenneth Clarke's original Civilisation series came out, Simon Schama, Mary Beard, and David Olusoga revisit the history of civilisation. M__

Coast - 2005 to 2016 - Each episode of this series takes a look at a bit of the coast in or near the British Isles. 1__ 2__ 3__ 4__ 5__ 6__ 7__ 8__ 9__ 10__ 11__

Coastal Railways with Julie Walters - 2017 - Julie Waters travels Britain's most scenic coastal railways, stopping off to visit the people and villages along the way. 1__

Countryfile - 1988 to present - This long-running weekly series celebrates rural life in the UK. While it doesn't truly have seasons, it's been running for 30 years. 1__ 2__ 3__ 4__ 5__ 6__ 7__ 8__ 9__ 10__ 11__ 12__ 13__ 14__ 15__ 16__ 17__ 18__ 19__ 20__ 21__ 22__ 23__ 24__ 25__ 26__ 27__ 28__ 29__ 30__

Country House Rescue - 2009 to 2012 - Businesswoman Ruth Watson helps struggling, crumbling country houses turn their fortunes around. 1__ 2__ 3__ 4__

Dan Cruickshank's Adventures in Architecture - 2008 - Dan Cruickshank travels around the world, showcasing many of its architectural treasures. M__

Don't Look Down - 2000 - This series takes a look at some of the most famous tall buildings in the UK. M__

Elizabeth I's Secret Agents - 2018 - Queen Elizabeth I was a protestant leader on the edge of a mostly Catholic content, in need of protection from the world's first secret service. M__

Escape to the Country - 2002 to present - Brits anxious to leave busy cities and suburbs look at properties and communities in the countryside. 1__ 2__ 3__ 4__ 5__ 6__ 7__ 8__ 9__ 10__ 11__ 12__ 13__ 14__ 15__

Europe's Roswell: UFO Crash at

Aberystwyth - 2009 - Mark Olly investigates a UFO sighting in Wales. M__

Extinct - 2001 - This documentary devotes six episodes to looking into the extinction of six animals. M__

Fake or Fortune - 2011 to 2017 - In each episode Fiona Bruce and Philip Mould examine a piece of artwork to help determine whether it's valuable or fake. 1__ 2__ 3__ 4__ 5__ 6__

Fantasy Homes by the Sea - 2007 to 2013 and 2018 to present - Each episode, Jenni Falconer takes prospective buyers to look at homes by the sea. 1__ 2__ 3__ 4__ 5__ 6__ | 1__

Flatpack Empire - 2018 - This documentary takes a behind-the-scenes look at IKEA. M__

Four in a Bed - 2010 to 2016 - Four B&B owners take turns staying at each other's establishments, then inspect and rate them. 1__ 2__ 3__ 4__ 5__ 6__ 7__ 8__ 9__ 10__

While Griff Rhys Jones is best known for his comedy roles, he's also an avid documentarian and very wealthy man after the sale of a production company he co-founded, Talkback.

Grand Tours of Scotland - 2010 to 2012 - Paul Murton explores many of Scotland's most scenic places. 1__ 2__ 3__ 4__ 5__ 6__ 7__

Grand Tours of Scotland's Lochs - 2017 to present - Scotland has over 30,000 lochs, and Paul Murton explores some of the most scenic and interesting of the group. 1__ 2__

Great British Garden Revival - 2013 to 2015 - Some of Britain's greatest horticultural talents aim to restore Britain's rich tradition of world-class gardens. 1__ 2__

Great British Railway Journeys - 2010 to 2018 - Michael Portillo explores Great Britain using the railways and his trusty Bradshaw Railway Guidebook. 1__ 2__ 3__ 4__ 5__ 6__ 7__ 8__ 9__

Great Canal Journeys - 2014 to present - Timothy West and his wife Prunella Scales travel the canals of Britain and beyond, enjoying adventures as long as her dementia will allow. 1__ 2__ 3__ 4__ 5__ 6__ 7__ 8__ 9__

Great Continental Railway Journeys - 2012 to 2018 - Michael Portillo travels across Europe using the 1913 Bradshaw Railway Guidebook to aide in his journey. 1__ 2__ 3__ 4__ 5__ 6__

Great Indian Railway Journeys - 2018 - Michael Portillo uses Bradshaw's 1913 handbook to travel across India. M__

Greatest Cities of the World - 2008 to 2010 - Griff Rhys Jones explores some of the world's most iconic cities. 1__ 2__

Griff's Great Britain - 2016 - Griff Rhys Jones explores the different types of terrain in Great Britain, stopping in towns and villages along the way. M___

Hidden Killers of the Victorian Home - 2013 - Suzannah Lipscomb takes a look at the hidden dangers that could have been deadly in Victorian homes. M___

How to Look at a Painting - 2011 - Justin Paton attempts to demystify art and help people better understand what they're looking at and why it matters. M___

How We Built Britain - 2007 to 2007 - This six-part series tells the story of Britain's architectural history. M___

In Search of Mr. Toad - 2013 - Griff Rhys Jones examines the life, times, and characters of Kenneth Grahame, author of "The Wind in the Willows". M___

Joanna Lumley in the Land of the Northern Lights - 2008 - Joanna tracks down the Northern Lights in the northern reaches of Norway. M___

Joanna Lumley's Greek Odyssey - 2011 to 2012 - Joanna Lumley visits the great historic sites of Greece. M___

Joanna Lumley's India - 2017 - Joanna visits the many treasured sites of India. M___

Joanna Lumley's Japan - 2016 - Joanna takes a 2000-mile trek across the four main islands of Japan. M___

Joanna Lumley's Silk Road Adventure - 2018 - Joanna Lumley (Absolutely Fabulous) embarks on a 7000-mile journey along the legendary Silk Road. M___

Joanna Lumley's Trans-Siberian Adventure - 2015 - Joanna Lumley travels on the Trans-Siberian Express from Hong Kong to Moscow. M___

Manor House aka The Edwardian Country House - 2002 - In this reality show, a group of people are given identities and placed in an elegant Scottish country house to live as Edwardians. M___

Martin Clune's Islands of Britain - 2009 - Martin Clunes explores the islands of Britain and meets some of the people who call them home. M___

Martin Clunes's Islands of Australia - 2016 - Martin Clunes explores some of the lesser-known islands off Australia's coast. M___

Michael Wood's Story of England - 2010 - Michael Wood tells the story of one village throughout English history. M___

Mortimer & Whitehouse: Gone Fishing - 2018 to present - Comedians and good friends embark on a journey fishing around Britain. 1___ 2___

Nothing Like a Dame - 2018 - Dames Judi Dench, Maggie Smith, Eileen Atkins, and Joan Plowright spend a weekend together at a country retreat, reflecting on the lives they've lived. M___

Penelope Keith At Her Majesty's Service - 2016 - Penelope travels to each of the Queen's four official residences in the UK .M___

Penelope Keith's Coastal Villages - 2018 to present - Penelope Keith travels the UK, visiting some of the most beautiful coastal villages. 1__

Penelope Keith's Hidden Villages - 2014 to 2016 - Penelope Keith takes us on a tour of the UK's loveliest villages and quirkiest characters. 1__ 2__ 3__

Princess Margaret: The Rebel Royal - 2018 - Princess Margaret embraced the social changes of the 60's and 70's and helps reshape the perception of the royal family. M__

Rivers by Jeremy Paxman - 2017 - Jeremy Paxman explores the great rivers of Britain and the people who live along them. M__

Rivers with Gryff Rhys Jones - 2009 - Actor and comedian Griff Rhys Jones explores the rivers of Britain and their history. M__

Robbie Coltrane Incredible Britain - 2007 to 2008 - Actor Robbie Coltrane (*Cracker*) road trips around Britain in his classic Jaguar roadster. M__

Robson Green's Coastal Lives - 2017 - Robson Green (*Grantchester*) takes us on a journey around some of Britain's most beautiful coastal destinations. M__

Secrets of the National Trust - 2017 to 2018 - Alan Titchmarsh travels the UK, gaining unprecedented access to a variety of historic properties. M__

Simon Schama: A History of Britain - 2002 - This massive, 15-part history of Britain begins around 3000 BC and ends at the year 2000 AD. M__

Sister Wendy's Odyssey - 1992 - Art expert and hermit Sister Wendy visits some of the world's great art galleries. M__

Station X - 1999 - Station X, Churchill's best-kept secret in Bletchley Park, was the center of codebreaking efforts in WWII. M__

Stephen Fry in America - 2008 to 2009 - Comedian and actor Stephen Fry embarks on a delightful romp around American in a black London cab. M__

Tales from Northumberland - 2013 to 2016 - Robson Green (*Grantchester*) takes us on a journey through his home county of Northumberland. 1__ 2__ 3__

The Art Detectives - 2017 to present - Art experts track down previously-unknown masterpieces by some of the world's greatest artists. 1__ 2__

The Churchills - 2012 - David Starkey looks at the links between Winston Churchill and his ancestor John Churchill, a man who dared to go up against Louis XIV of France. M__

The Country House Revealed - 2011 - Dan Cruickshank goes behind the scenes in six of Britain's greatest private homes. M__

The Curious Houseguest - 2005 to 2006 - In each episode, historian and journalist Jeremy Musson visits a historic home. 1__ 2__

The Investigator: A British Crime

Story - 2016 - This documentary series follows a different real-life missing persons case in each season. 1___ 2___

The Life and Times of the Real Robyn Hoode - 2015 - This feature-length documentary attempts to separate fact from fiction with respect to the legendary outlaw. M___

The Lost Gardens of Heligan - 2014 - The Lost Gardens of Heligan were beautiful until WWI, and this program takes a look at the efforts to restore this Cornish site to its former glory. M___

The Magic of Houdini - 2014 - Alan Davies talks about the magic of Houdini and some of the magicians he's influenced. M___

The Plantagenets - 2014 - Professor Robert Bartlett explores the history of one of England's bloodiest and longest-lasting dynasties. M___

The World's Most Extraordinary Homes - 2017 to present - Architect Piers Taylor and actress Caroline Quentin tour the world in search of its most incredible homes. 1___ 2___

The World's Most Famous Train - 2015 - This documentary follows 40 staff members and 180 passengers as they make the 36-hour across Europe on the Venice Simplon-Orient-Express. M___

The Yorkshire Vet - 2015 to present - This engaging series follows the staff of Skeldale Veterinary Centre as they work with the animals. 1___ 2___ 3___ 4___ 5___ 6___ 7___

Three Men in a Boat - 2006 - Griff Rhys Jones brings two comedian friends along for a boat journey around Britain. M___

Time Team - 1994 to 2014 - A group of archaeologists travel around Britain working on different excavation sites. 1___ 2___ 3___ 4___ 5___ 6___ 7___ 8___ 9___ 10___ 11___ 12___ 13___ 14___ 15___ 16___ 17___ 18___ 19___ 20___

Tony Robinson's Coast to Coast - 2017 - Tony travels from coast to coast in Britain, stopping off at scenic and historic places along the way. M___

Travel Man - 2015 to present - In each episode, Richard Ayoade and a guest pick a different city to visit for 48 hours. 1___ 2___ 3___ 4___ 5___ 6___ 7___ 8___

Treats from the Edwardian Country House - 2002 - Chef Hugh Fearnley-Whittingstall looks at the food they would have served during the Edwardian era. M___

Victorian Bakers - 2016 - Four modern bakers experience what it was like to bake in Victorian times. 1___

Vintage Roads: Great & Small - 2018 - Christopher and Timothy travel along Britain's vintage roads in a 1936 Morgan 4/4. 1___

Walking Through History - 2013 to 2015 - Tony Robinson selects walking routes around Britain for their ability to showcase history. 1___ 2___ 3___ 4___

Walks With My Dog - 2016 - Celebrities take their dogs on walks around some of Britain's most stunning scenery. 1___

Who Do You Think You Are? - 2004 to present - Celebrities get a peek into their family histories to answer questions about themselves. 1___ 2___ 3___ 4___ 5___ 6___ 7___ 8___ 9___ 10___ 11___ 12___ 13___ 14___ 15___

Wild Britain With Hugh Bonneville - 2018 - Hugh narrates this series about the plants, animals, and ecosystems of Great Britain. M___

MY NOTES

AUSTRALIAN

THE HEART GUY (1-3)

MYSTERY ROAD

DOCUMENTARIES

SOUNDBREAKING

This interview originally appeared in Issue 3 of the Acorn TV Dispatch in May 2018. It is reprinted here with permission.

Nettles played DCI Tom Barnaby in the first 81 episodes of ***Midsomer Murders***. Read on to see what he has to say about *Midsomer*'s popularity in the United States, what he's up to now, and what he misses most about the series — then catch up on the all-new season of *Midsomer Murders*, now streaming on **Acorn TV**!

How do you explain the appeal of *Midsomer Murders* in the U.S.?

I think it's very popular in the USA because it is quintessentially English. And the Americans love nothing better than looking at us, the old colonial power, and enjoying the Englishness of it all.

I get a lot of mail from America, about which I'm very pleased. I once got a letter from the chief of police in Chicago, who said he admired Barnaby's methodology and that he himself used to follow that line of investigation when he was on a case. And I have a letter from a calligraphy expert at an American university talking about using calligraphy as an indication of what kind of character you are. I sent her some of my writing, and she said that I was a self-centered, egocentric actor, probably – which is right!

***Midsomer Murders* has had many well-known guest stars over the years. Which of them stand out for you?**

The main ones I remember are Alan Howard, one of the greatest English classical actors, and Donald Sinden, who was never understated about anything – he was the most extraordinary man. And Richard Briers, who was in his 60s when he appeared in one of our episodes. Despite not being in the best of health, he wanted to do all of his own stunts – including, as he put it, "leaping like a gazelle" to the top of a church tower. He was prevented from doing so, of course, but it was a close-run thing.

There were also many wonderful women – Renée Asherson, for example, who played Ophelia in Laurence Olivier's *Hamlet*. I remember that incredibly iconic first scene of "The Killings at Badger's Drift," riding her bike through the typically English village. Many other brilliant female actresses appeared in *Midsomer Murders*. Mary Wimbush is one. Angela Down, who produced the most extraordinary performance in "Blue Herrings," is another. And Elizabeth Spriggs, of course, also in "The Killings at Badger's Drift." The list is endless.

What do you miss most about what was such a big part of your life for so long?

I miss not having to cook my own breakfast, lunch, and tea. I was fairly institutionalized when I was on *Midsomer Murders* – I was picked up every morning, dressed, and then taken to the set. I liked that lifestyle!

In all seriousness, though, what I missed most when I left was the camaraderie of the set – everyone there together, bringing this extraordinary show to the screen. There was an element of family amongst us, and I was very fond of everyone involved in it. To a man they were wonderful people. *And* I miss the money!

Are you working on any projects now? Anything our Acorn TV viewers might look forward to?

At the moment I'm working on a TV documentary about the Channel Islands. I worked there when I was on [the detective series] *Bergerac* and found it an absolutely extraordinary place. I've since written two books about the Channel Islands, one of which is actually translated into German and, I think, is available in the USA.

I've done a turn in *Poldark* – I'm Cornish, so I was quite happy to do a program that was set in Cornwall. I'm also publishing a wartime diary from someone who lived in the Channel Islands during the war. It's one of the best diaries of the war I have ever read, and I came across it in 2012 while working on a documentary. It's just an incredible commentary on the war as a whole, written in relation to all of the events on the islands at the time.

Though the series has always been an Acorn TV fan favorite, there may be a few viewers who haven't seen it yet. If you had to pick one episode, which would you recommend?

My favorite episode is "Blue Herrings," which was set in an old people's home. We went down to Denville Hall, which is a home for old actresses, [who] taught us youngsters a few things! There's one extraordinary performance in it from Angela Down, who gave the most moving and incredibly detailed performance. It was by some distance the best-ever performance in *Midsomer Murders*.

The episode had a funny side as well, because it was the only episode that didn't actually feature a murder. It was called "Blue Herrings," which is just incredibly witty. And this wittiness in the episode just makes it a really lovely thing to watch.

WHERE TO WATCH BRITISH TV

While your options for finding British programming will vary based on your location, North American readers will generally have good luck with the services below. Some are available in other countries.

For links and more information on each service, visit our website at:

IHeartBritishTV.com/services

ACORN TV

Acorn TV has been around for several years, and they have a solid menu British programming - generally around 250-270 titles in total, give or take a couple dozen.

What's different about Acorn TV is that while they specialize in British TV, they also have programming from Ireland, Canada, Australia, New Zealand, and mainland Europe.

BRITBOX

BritBox came out in 2017, but they're no strangers to British TV. The service is co-owned by the BBC and ITV, two of the biggest forces in UK television. They average around 300 titles in total, give or take a couple dozen depending on when you check.

BritBox is slightly more expensive than Acorn TV, but they do give you access to a lot of content you can't get any other legal way. They offer next-day viewing for the major British soap operas, and they have a number of panel shows (like QI) and live events (like the Edinburgh Military Tattoo).

There is very little overlap between Acorn TV & BritBox (we'd estimate less than 5%).

PBS MASTERPIECE

While your standard local PBS is a great source of British programming, they also offer a channel on Amazon Video. It's very heavy on period dramas, and they also offer quite a bit of non-English international programming through Walter Presents (roughly 300 hours at publication time).

NETFLIX

At any given time, you can find somewhere between 100-200 British TV shows and another 100+ British movies on Netflix. Note that this is just an estimate based on recent counts, and it could change at any time.

To view lists of British shows and movies on Netflix, visit IHeartBritishTV.com/netflix.

AMAZON VIDEO

If you have an Amazon Prime membership for the free shipping benefits, you may be overlooking a great source of British television. At our last count, there were more than 160 British TV shows on Prime Video.

To view a list of British shows available with a Prime membership, visit IHeartBritishTV.com/amazon

HULU

Since a lot of people think of Hulu as a replacement for traditional TV, they're often surprised to learn that Hulu actually has a healthy collection of British TV shows – many of which aren't available with any other streaming subscriptions.

To view a list of British TV shows available on Hulu, visit IHeartBritishTV.com/hulu

SUNDANCE NOW

Sundance Now usually offers 10-20 British programs and a few Australian or Canadian titles. Many are high-profile series like McMafia and The Split.

CINEMAX

Cinemax doesn't have a lot of British titles, but they do get the occasional high-profile series like C.B. Strike or Rellik.

STARZ

Starz is another premium channel with a handful of high-profile titles. In recent months, they've offered Outlander, The White Queen, and Apple Tree Yard.

SHOWTIME

Showtime has a handful of British titles at most times, and recent years have seen them offering Patrick Melrose, The Tudors, Episodes, and Penny Dreadful.

BEST OF BRITISH TELEVISION

Best of British Television is an Amazon channel that primarily offers British reality television.

TUBI.TV

Tubi.TV is a free, ad-supported, and most importantly, legal service that allows you to stream some British TV shows without paying a subscription fee.

YOUR LOCAL LIBRARY

If your budget is tight, check with your local library. They may use services like Kanopy or Hoopla to make some TV shows available at no charge. Others offer DVDs for rental.

DVDS

When nothing else has a show you want, try DVDs. More popular shows are generally released on Region 1 (North American) DVDs, but others are only available on Region 2 (UK/European) DVDs.

Ordering DVDs From the UK

MANY SHOWS ARE ONLY AVAILABLE ON REGION 2 DVDS

- **To play UK DVDs (Region 2 DVDs), North American viewers will need a "Region-Free" (or All-Region) DVD Player**
- **You can get a region-free DVD player on sites like Amazon or eBay, but not in big box stores.**
- **Some computer DVD drives will also play Region 2 DVDs**

For more information about regional DVD restrictions, visit IHeartBritishTV.com/DVDS

HOW TO STREAM TO YOUR TELEVISION

If you've been watching services like Acorn TV and BritBox on your laptop or computer because you don't know how to get them on your television, let me assure you - there's an easy fix.

Much like VCRs and DVD players plug into your television, there's a similar option for streaming media. Actually, there are several, but we're keeping this simple.

For as little as $30, you can get a Roku device that works with your TV and internet to bring content to your screen. There are no smart TV compatibility issues to worry about, and they're easy to use.

Want to know more? We have a tutorial at IHeartBritishTV.com/ROKU

CONTRIBUTORS

TOBY O'BRIEN

VERENA ROSE

KATHY O'DONNELL

VERA LANDE

SHERRI DAVIS

ALISON HEFFES

We greatly appreciate your early contributions in getting this guide published!

Special thanks to Acorn TV for allowing us to include the John Nettles interview.

Additional thanks to Liberty White for your contributions to IHeartBritishTV.com and the I Heart British TV Facebook group.

FIND US ONLINE

Online At:

IHeartBritishTV.com

IHeartBritain.com

Facebook:

Facebook.com/IHeartBritishTV

Facebook.com/IHeartBritain

Instagram:

Instagram.com/IHeartBritishTV

Instagram.com/IHeartBritaindotcom

Pinterest:

Pinterest.com/IHeartBritaindotcom

Our Store:

Shop.IHeartBritain.com

Want to know more? We have a tutorial at IHeartBritishTV.com/ROKU

CPSIA information can be obtained
at www.ICGtesting.com
Printed in the USA
FSHW011416300119
55348FS